THE CHILDREN ON THE HILL

THE CHILDREN
ON THE HILL

*One Family's Bold Experiment
with a New Way of Learning and Growing*

by Michael Deakin

THE BOBBS-MERRILL COMPANY, INC.
Indianapolis / New York

ISBN 0-672-51843-0
Library of Congress Catalog Card Number: 73-1731
Manufactured in the United States of America

First printing

CONTENTS

Maria and her family were the subject of Yorkshire Television's highly successful network documentary film, *Shows Promise – Should Go Far*, and some of the material in this book was gathered in the course of making this programme.

Dr Anna Cecil of Cambridge University offered much valuable advice on the genetic aspects of genius, and Cindy Woodward and Lilian Wilkinson helped in the preparation of the book. Maurice King and Robin Constable provided hospitality and encouragement.

The author is grateful to them all.

MD

CHAPTER ONE

THE FAMILY

The voice at the other end of the telephone was apologising.

'The house is very untidy,' it said. 'It's a long way out of town. It really isn't fit to be seen. It's all shabby and untidy.'

The line was poor and the person at the other end spoke with a strange lilting accent that was hard to place.

'Don't worry,' I protested, professionally soothing, 'you should see my house. It's amazingly untidy too.'

The voice at the other end of the line sounded doubtful.

'I don't know why you want to come – there's very little for you to see. Nothing out of the ordinary.'

More protests followed and then a gradual concession. An appointment was made. In my office three hundred miles away train time-tables were looked out, and maps were found. The Welsh village which I had been calling was far away in a remote corner of the principality, and connections were impossibly difficult and slow. The only train went through London and would take hours. The whole project seemed like an imposition – but there was nobody else to go. Grudgingly and carrying a few clothes, I set off.

My television company was working on a series of international exchange programmes. A film devoted to gifted children was being made simultaneously in a number of countries. Doubtless the Russians were at this very moment seeking out and filming future Grand Masters of chess, the Japanese were testing junior karate champions and the Americans were analysing the offspring of the space scientists at Cape Kennedy. As always with international ventures there was an underlying sense of competition and a slight chauvinistic desire to show off the prowess of British television and childhood alike.

The purpose of my long journey in the depths of winter: in this particular Welsh village there was said to be a child pianist of genius. A year ago, when he was only nine, he had appeared briefly at a contest and then disappeared again as quickly. Everybody in the music world knew about him but nobody seemed to know exactly where he had gone. It was an intriguing story and a possible candidate for our film, and after some research we had succeeded in locating the family in their remote home. International programmes are expensive, prestige films allow no mistakes, so here I was going to find out exactly who this child was, to explore his life in his remote Welsh village.

Pausing in London only to buy a fashionable pair of patent leather boots, I resentfully caught the train to Wales and enveloping hours later was peering out of the window at the deep snow which was falling heavily, palling the unfamiliar Welsh countryside. London seemed a lifetime away, the journey truly endless. The village where the musical child lived was quite literally the end of the line, to be reached only after passing a sad procession of gaunt coal mines—the train rattling past their black slag heaps prettified with a coating of untrodden snow, topped by derricks standing like iron lace against the dull grey sky.

For the last half-hour of the journey the carriage was empty and the game of trying to pronounce the station name-boards was the only diversion in a trip so long that all reading matter had been exhausted. The end came at last. A single stooped, deaf Welsh porter took the ticket. I looked around. There was nobody there to meet me, as had been promised. I was left alone, standing on the heavy splintering planks of the platform, the giant flakes of Welsh snow falling heavily onto my new patent leather boots. Already they were leaking heartily, boding ill for twenty-four hours doomed to be spent with squelching feet.

Ten minutes passed. Then another ten minutes. I looked at the address – a string of incomprehensible Welsh words on a scrap of paper. Should one try it on foot in the deserted frozen town? It shouldn't be too difficult. Already I had a vision in my mind's eye of what awaited me. A cheerful terraced house, a piano in the front room. Father a healthy miner – a member of the local male voice choir – much singing of Land of My Fathers. They would be simple Orwellian Welsh folk, coming singing home in the evening from the mine, their faces shining black with coal dust, and taking a bath in a tub in front of a roaring fire . . . .

'Mr Deakin.' The voice was very gentle, educated and reedy.

I turned round. In the snow by the station arch stood a figure so totally unlike the hearty singing miner I had expected, that my breath was momentarily taken away: a gentle stooping figure in a knee-length fawn raincoat. A long tangled black beard fringed the stern Rabbinical face that peered out from under long black hair. Only his brown eyes were soft and very very gentle. In one hand he held an umbrella, his fingers shrouded by thick black woollen mittens, newly knitted. I stared. A stranger figure to step out of a Welsh blizzard would have been hard to imagine. Surprise made me hearty.

'Jolly nice of you to meet me,' said I. 'Let's just grab a taxi – it's no weather for walking.'

'Don't think you will be able to persuade a taxi to go where I live.'

'Oh?'

'It's a fair way.'

I looked out into the swirling snow.

'But we can take a bus some of the way.'

We plunged into the town. Not a soul was forth and the snow was driving parallel to the ground, finding even the smallest gaps in clothing, eager to penetrate. We arrived at the deserted bus station and sat in the bus – just the two of us – waiting, shivering, for a driver and conductor courageous enough to set off into the blizzard. Pools of water began to gather on the bus floor as the snow melted off our clothing. The bearded man smiled and nodded and smiled again, but conversation became sparser and sparser. The conductor and driver arrived, talking loudly in Welsh. Eerily the bus set off into the blizzard.

Soon the lighted shop windows were left behind, then the houses, and the bus began to climb into the snow-flecked darkness. Somehow London and the chatter of the television studios seemed very far away.

The bus stopped.

'This is as far as we go,' the conductor said. We stepped out into a driving wall of snow, below us the intermittent winking of the town lights.

'There's still quite a walk from here,' said my companion in his reedy voice, as we set off into the unknown.

We passed some scattered cottages and went into what seemed, under its blanket of snow, to be a ploughed field. Stumbling, I fell cursing into a ditch, filling my patent leather boots with snow and completing their leaky discomfort. Three or four sheep were sheltering uncomfortably under a stone wall. Stooping forward, we climbed on. By now I was regretting every icy step, wishing myself warm and safe in London. We breasted a small rise, and there below us was a stone cottage standing fully exposed in the path of the storm. Around it, as though for warmth, huddled several seemingly derelict outhouses and half demolished walls. A light was on upstairs and from the window a yellow beam fell across the snow as though in a fairytale. Somebody was playing Mozart on the piano and the sound came pure and perfect over the snow. For a moment I thought it must be a gramophone or the wireless, but at the end of a movement the pianist started again at the beginning without faltering. It was a moment of pure magic.

Showing off, I said. 'That sounds like K.488.'

'I don't know, perhaps you are right,' came the reply as we bent into the snow. Cold, wet, tired and cross though I was, I didn't want this spell to break as we trudged the last hundred yards towards the cottage. As if in response to the magic, as we approached, there was a sudden lull in the storm and our feet were silent in the deep snow almost as though they too didn't want to interrupt the playing.

Past a row of silent disapproving hens fluffed up behind a wall, and we were there. My companion opened the simple wooden door which stood secured only by a latch. No sooner ajar than it escaped his hand and tore open, admitting a flurry of snow with us. After the climb and the musical spell woven on the snow outside, it took time to become adjusted to indoors, and we stood puffing and dripping just inside the door.

An ill-tempered cat was scooped off a chair, and I sat down and began to look around me. The room was astonishing. At first glance it looked as though its contents had been stirred by a giant who had then gone off in a huff leaving everything higgledy-piggledy. But on further examination it became apparent that there was perfect order everywhere. It was a children's room. Everything had been done to make it full of adventure and excitement. Every available inch of wall space was covered with paintings or drawings so that the mundane pattern of the wallpaper was all but invisible. Every inch of shelf or mantelpiece was piled with curiously shaped stones, little bunches of grass, plants growing in paper cups, glittering pieces of glass or hand-wrought models. Here was a room from which nothing had ever been thrown away, in which nobody had been told 'don't bring that in here, it's dirty'. It wasn't a room designed and set up for children by adults, but a room on which children had impressed themselves till it was truly theirs. It was quite unlike anything I had seen before. And all the while I was taking stock, the sound of the piano filled the room.

The unseen player – it must be the boy I'd come to see –

neither faltered nor changed with the commotion of a visitor. Below, our conversation was punctuated by the silvery sounds of the Mozart sonata he was now playing.

The woman who had apologised on the telephone was greeting me, apologising in turn for the disorder, for the walk, for the weather. She was small, her hair drawn tightly into a bun behind her head, her face a perfect creamy oval, her eyes a deep brown with a slightly startled expression. No sooner did one see her than it was apparent why her voice seemed strange: she was Italian. Hers was the face of scores of Madonnas in paintings all over Italy. Her accent, heavily overlaid with Welsh and her confusion, was as Italian as her face.

Sitting round a kitchen table that filled a corner of the room, were three children. The eldest – a boy of about eleven – was so absorbed in the school books in front of him that apart from a distant 'hello' he scarcely seemed to be aware of my intrusion. But even the two words he spoke showed that his accent mirrored perfectly that of his mother. Next to him was a girl with her mother's perfect oval face, who was painting – a dozen pots of brightly coloured model aircraft paints were lined up in front of her. She was smiling welcomingly. A ravishing child of about four or five completed the trio. His cheeks were scarlet, his eyes blue and his mop of fair hair covered a surprisingly high domed forehead. Unlike his brother and sister he seemed neither shy nor reserved. On the contrary, as soon as we were through the door he demanded the attention of his father for the picture he was working on, and the slightly stooping figure went over to his son, the corners of his brown eyes crinkling up as he took the child onto his lap. It was an extraordinarily gentle and peaceful gesture. Clearly the child and his father sat like this every evening. One sensed no barrier between them, no reserve or dissimulation at all.

A glance around confirmed that there was no television, apparently no radio, no comics and none of the paraphernalia of broken pistols and rusting sheriff's badges so often kept to entertain small children. In spite of my presence, father and child were so engrossed in their chosen occupations, and with such a deep absorption, that I might hardly have been there.

The mother introduced herself as Maria and gave me a cup of tea. I became aware that the house wasn't warm – a fire burnt in the grate but it was unable to do much against the raging cold outside or the wind that took possession of the windows and doors and rattled their ill-fitting frames. Upstairs the piano playing continued, never faltering, with never a wrong note, as perfect as though somebody was giving a concert.

I asked if I might go upstairs, stepped over a dozen assorted gumboots and a discarded tricycle, and stumbled up a dark low stairway built hundreds of years ago for a dwarf Welshman.

The music came from a room to the left: I opened the door. Inside, his back to the door, sat a tiny child. The first shock was his smallness, his slippered feet dangling an inch or so from the pedals, his head barely appearing above the top of the upright piano.

'Hello,' I said bravely.

Reluctantly the child took his hands from the keyboard.

'Hello,' he said.

'Well, what are you doing?'

'Playing. . . .' there was a long pause, '. . . the piano.'

His high thin voice seemed to come from about three feet behind his head. He regarded me gravely with enormous dark eyes. I tried again.

'Do you like Mozart?'

No reply.

'Or do you like Beethoven better?'

He continued to regard me gravely. Then he pursed his lips, made as if to speak, thought better of it and took up gazing again. A last try – 'What do you think about,' I asked, 'while you play?'

'The music,' the child said.

I retreated downstairs, confused. Before I had closed the door he had begun to play again.

Downstairs, the eldest boy looked up from his books.

'I'm stuck with this question,' he said, 'can you help me?'

Here at least one was on safe ground. The child was visibly only eleven. I could see he was doing some sort of arithmetic. I went over to the table. There, on the paper the child was working on, was a sea of equations. Some of them were joined together by squiggly vertical lines making triple decked equations, others were linked by symbols I only dimly remembered from other students' textbooks at University. I thought I recognised a piece of differential calculus. Was it a joke? I looked sharply at the child, who regarded me as gravely as his brother had done, no trace of a joke in his eyes: there could be no honourable escape. I said desperately: 'I don't think I can help, I'm afraid.' But before I left the table I saw the full beauty of the dazzling paintings the absorbed girl was creating. And as I passed her younger brother I noticed that the four-year-old was working on a piece of Euclidian geometry which even I knew was premature at his age.

Later that night in a cold commercial hotel where dinner stopped at seven, and unobtainable shilling pieces were needed for the gas, I realised that on that snowy hill one of the strangest stories I had ever encountered was being played out.

These grave self-possessed children were almost like a piece of science fiction. Were they all as clever as they seemed? Had they been born so gifted or was there something in the heavily charged atmosphere of that cottage that had made them so evidently advanced? How had they come to be on that remote hillside in Wales? Did anybody from the out-side world fully realise what was happening? Far away from metropolitan normality I almost began to doubt the strange scene on the hill which I had so recently experienced.

Further acquaintance with the family showed that the story was as fascinating as first impressions had indicated. The austere isolation they lived in had been deliberately chosen to provide an environment suited to bringing up the children, and far from being the result of a benevolent accident, the children's gifts were apparently the result of a deliberate and unique educational plan. Like all stories of families, it is one which starts way back, in the childhood of the mother. And before one can understand and discuss her attitudes or her achievements, one must know what kind of person she is, and how she arrived at the extraordinary decisions she has taken.

CHAPTER TWO

MARIA

Maria was born in Perugia, a town set in one of the most beautiful parts of central Italy. Site of a medieval university, it stands perched on the hills looking out over the yellow plains. But Maria's childhood was spent in southern Italy, where her father, an officer in the Italian Navy, was stationed. There the land is flat, often arid and uninviting, with stones scattered over the dry fields as though in an abandoned cemetery. It was here, in Brescia, that Maria's brother was born, and here that her beautiful mother died giving birth to him. It was the beginning of a lonely and often unhappy childhood.

Maria's father was kind to his children, but his professional preoccupations kept him away from them a great deal and too often they were left in the care of servants and friends. Yet there were summer evenings, at dusk after the last notes of the bugle which sounded the curfew had died away, when he would sit with his grave-eyed daughter and tiny son reading them mystical poems – sometimes passing hours declaiming the works of Tagore. To Maria these verses seemed mysterious but fascinating, full of strange and sweet images.

But life with Maria's father was not all poetry. His daughter had an exceptionally strong will and often suffered from fears which seemed to him irrational, and he saw it as his duty to constrain the former and help her overcome the latter. For instance, the child was afraid of the dark, especially in the open countryside around their home. Her father would take her out into the nocturnal woods and command her to walk forward into the darkness until he gave the order to turn back. Her heart thumping in real fear of some supernatural presence, she would edge forward, waiting sometimes for upwards of ten minutes before she was allowed to stop and could come running back to the protective arms of her stern father. But her fear was not wholly irrational, it was born of insecurity and a sense of being rejected. The loss of her mother made the former inevitable; her father, often unwittingly, contributed to the latter.

Maria was rejected for every childish misbehaviour. As a punishment her father would pretend to cast her out from his affection. 'Daughter?' he would say, 'I have no daughter. Who are you?'

Desperately the child would try to gain some recognition from him, to secure his forgiveness, only to be repeatedly rebuffed until the punishment had run the course he had set for it. As he was otherwise often tender and affectionate, and Maria was devoted to him, these strange punishments were deeply disturbing and could only increase her sense of insecurity and unworthiness. This in turn led to renewed displays of will and further inevitable retribution. It was a depressing and oft repeated cycle.

Maria's father's duties became more and more pressing and he spent much of his time on his ship. The children were left to a governess. For Maria this proved to be little short of a disaster. She was an intelligent child who asked even more, and more searching, questions than most children, and irritated by this the governess resorted to the simple expedient of locking the child in an empty room for hour after hour, leaving her only an ABC book to read – telling her to shut up, and get on with learning it. While this effectively stemmed the barrage of questions and left the woman free to do whatever else she fancied, it damaged the child terribly. Confined in the room she would gaze at the book, trying to make sense out of the incomprehensible characters, then give way to endless mumbling, boredom and despair, her mind softening when it should have been at its sharpest. So great was the governess's neglect that Maria reached her eighth birthday unable to read and write.

Then war broke out; her father was ordered to sea. Maria and her brother, Alberto, were rescued from this tartar by their grandparents and taken back to Perugia, which was further away from the fighting and thus felt to be safer.

Maria's grandparents were among the richest and most influential bourgeoisie of the city. The house in which they lived was large and austere, the hangings dark, substantial, and made to last. The children were not allowed to run about or make any unseemly noise in the house, the whole of which was pervaded, as one visitor said, 'with a very special doom'. But the children were secure, and their grandparents' ordered and regular lives provided a framework within which Maria could come to terms once more with the normal realities of childhood. Once more she started asking the questions which previously had gone without answer, first asking them of herself, then of the books which now surrounded her in liberal profusion. As soon as she was able to read, she found that there was always a ready answer available from the obliging printed page. Words themselves fascinated her and gave her a sense of security, their meaning complex but unchanging – and however close she got to their secrets they made no emotional demands of her.

This part of Maria's childhood contained other pleasures, too, beside that of starting to use her mind. It was by no means wholly arid. The countryside was beautiful, and she and her brother spent days collecting plants and flowers, enjoying the delights of living in such a lovely place, and sometimes, as a special treat, being taken to nearby Assisi to look at a Giotto painting in a church there. For almost the first time Maria and Alberto were happy.

Soon, however, their father was reported missing, then dead: another terrible blow to the two children. Huddled together, they would often simply dissolve into tears at the very thought of the sorrow and deprivation that had always seemed to be their lot. Withdrawing into themselves they began to play new games. When they grew up they would have a house together, and would live together; they would have each other whatever else might befall. Already Maria, older and more cruelly affected by the previous disasters, felt that somehow she didn't belong – didn't belong with people of her own age, didn't belong with her grandparents. Only in her younger brother, handsome and devoted, did she feel that she had any being at all.

So it was through her brother that she now set out to live. She would work for her grandmother, embroidering and suchlike, so that she should have money to give to him. He would set his heart on some new plaything or garment, such as a dashing pair of swimming trunks, and his devoted sister would save up her pocket-money and forego every small luxury until he had his desire. Visitors would come to the house and admire the boy with cries of 'How good-looking he is, how beautiful'. In her deepest heart his sister believed it to be true, felt sure that she was as nothing beside this wonderful brother of hers.

But in one sphere Maria seemed to have begun to come into her own: school. Although she had remained almost totally illiterate till she was eight, now she was bounding through her school work. Of course, it was a Fascist school – the words 'Credere, Obbedire, Combattere' ('Believe, Obey, Fight') were hung on the class-room wall, and there was the usual quota of prayers for the Duce, loyalty parades and patriotic duties. But in this respect the children's grandmother showed a proud determination. She went down to the school, saw the headmistress, and brow-beat her into allowing her grandchildren to forgo the Fascist indoctrination.

These problems apart, in school Maria suddenly found herself catapulted into a world full of interest. She took to learning like a duck to water, often occupying herself for pleasure with the most demanding and driest subjects, such as classical Greek and philology. Words still fascinated her, their cold and logical discipline seeming a way of escaping the necessity of coming to grips with the more immediate and dangerously emotional life outside.

By the time she was sixteen, Maria was studying furiously, staying up every night till about 3 am, trying to prove herself to herself, to show herself that she could understand, could keep in front of the others. Unfortunately her grandparents were both unsympathetic and unimpressed.

'You are only an orphan,' they said, 'and furthermore a girl orphan. We may die and then there won't be any money for you to go to university. You must get a practical qualification – for instance that of a nurse.' It represented a practical and cautious view, in tune with their old-fashioned way of life. But all the girl wanted to do was to study – she was consumed with the desire for education as though by fire. In the end it was her teacher who went and persuaded the grandparents to let her continue with her studies, convincing them of their grand-daughter's outstanding aptitude and the public shame of forcing so talented a child to give up her education.

It was at this time that Maria fell in love for the first time. Her choice: her Latin teacher, an 'absolutely ugly' man, devoted to the Catholic Church, to which he repaired two or three times a day. Since his religious duties took up so much of his time, and Maria's scholarly ones so much of hers, their friendship was not destined to flourish. He married somebody else. Maria was heartbroken, and her grandparents resolved to send her to Rome University, where she was to take a degree not, as she would have wished, in philosophy, but in Greek philology. To prevent any recurrence of amatory troubles she was lodged in a convent of Spanish nuns. This suited her, since she was now going through the intense religious phase common in adolescence, and was contemplating becoming a nun herself.

Whatever the future might hold, she was now free to devote her full energies and pronounced willpower to her studies, and this she did with a characteristically wholehearted application. Not content with the bare syllabus, she spent all her days in the library reading through subjects which lay at a tangent, devouring everything that came her way. After a while she began to have doubts about her religious life, and to spend hours wrestling on points of doctrine with the Chaplain of the Spanish convent. Characteristically she explored the dogma of the Catholic Church as fully as possible before deciding that she was unable to accept it, and leaving the Church. Despairingly the priest told her, rightly, that she was very strong, if not for good then for evil.

Also characteristically, she decided to stay on in the convent, a situation which must, since she had left the Church, have been fraught with embarrassment both for the pious sisters and for herself. Her intense scholarly life left little time for the gay social life of Rome University, and anyhow she was now beginning to feel a good deal of distrust for such things; but she made many friends among the serious-minded girls who, like herself, spent their time in the library and lecture theatre, rather than at 'surprise parties' and the beach.

This austerity was a reflection of her 'outsider' temperament even in the world of the university she had so longed to join, and it was also an apparent demonstration of the way she was slowly drifting further and further away from her adored brother. His tastes now ran firmly with those of the bourgeoisie of Perugia with whom, by virtue of wealth and birth, he now mixed; and while he still talked of their shared fantasy of a joint home, he had started to spend much of his time with girl friends, or at dances. Furthermore, unlike his sister, he saw nothing wrong in enjoying inherited wealth, and bought himself first a scooter and then a car as soon as he was able.

To begin with Maria had believed that her abstract studies would somehow enable her to understand the central meaning of life. Gradually she began to realise that before any comprehension of life was possible she would have to participate in it, and that furthermore she would have to do so in the strongest possible way. She therefore firmly divested herself of the social privileges she had anyhow always felt to be wrong, and threw herself with all the determination bred of a strong will into what she felt to be good works. Much of her spare time was now spent working for Danilo Dolci, the Sicilian social reformer, long before it became fashionable to espouse his cause. It was as though, by allying herself with the poor and with those set outside society, she hoped that somehow she would gain an identity for herself.

It was now that she met Martin. He too was at Rome University, but he was totally unlike the boys she was used to and she was fascinated by him. He was a foreigner, Jewish and apart. He moved through the university, stooping and gentle, with his mind on the social problems that surrounded him rather than on the latest hit record. Already Martin had visited and lived in several other countries. He was far older in himself than his contemporaries – and, in sharp contrast to the fashionable young men of Perugia, he was poor and shabby. For Maria this new friend came as a draught of fresh air, for not only was he different from all the people she had found so vapid, but he was also prepared – anxious in fact – to take her and her thoughts seriously. They talked for hours about fundamentals, Martin listening gravely and gently, and in their spare moments they worked for Dolci, printing and distributing leaflets. They talked much of God and religion, and Maria and Martin both began, as they put it, to feel that 'reality was coming to us, by our being together'. Both of them archetypal 'outsiders', in each other they found a bastion against a world governed by motives and considerations which they themselves could not accept.

When Maria announced to her grandparents that she was engaged to be married to this strange shabby foreigner, they were horror-struck. Obviously he was an adventurer after her money; or worse, he was an enthraller of helpless girls.

24

They opposed the match passionately, bringing into play all the weapons open to a powerful bourgeois family in Italy. Martin's residence permit was questioned, Maria's allowance cut off. But strong willed as her grandmother was, she was no match for the equally marked determination of her grand-daughter. Maria declined to take any further financial support from her family and moved away from the convent. Times became very hard – she and Martin had almost no money, too little food, holes in their shoes, and that year's winter in Rome was terribly cold.

Maria gave Latin and Greek lessons, but there was still pitifully little money.

Nevertheless, the two lovers felt strong in each other, like two characters from Bunyan. Nor was the comparison so far-fetched, since they themselves felt that their relationship had about it a sense of captured reality. Such things were, of course, totally beyond the comprehension of her grand-parents surrounded by 'the special doom' of their great dark house in Perugia. Nor were tensions lessened by the fact that her beloved brother Alberto also felt hostile to this strange, unprepossessing foreigner who seemed to be about to sweep away his sister.

Maria responded by opting out of their world, losing herself in Martin, their talk and their social crusade. Then the mother of a college friend took pity on her and offered her a roof over her head and above all approval and support. Gratefully she accepted. She was unable to pay any rent but it was agreed she would repay one day when things were easier.

It was hard to see when this would happen. Maria's family reacted increasingly hysterically to what they saw simply as a classic case of infatuation. Now it was Martin who became stubborn, showing the refusal to compromise that lay beneath his gentle exterior. 'You must choose' he said, 'between your family and me. Once you start to compromise there will be no peace left, and all will be destroyed between us.' He issued a direct ultimatum, announced they were to go to England and that he had fixed the date: March 28th 1957.

On the appointed day they left, having put on wedding rings bought with their last savings: a symbolic gesture that they hoped would give them extra courage. As they travelled northwards, Maria became aware, almost for the first time, of the full power of the taboos they had broken. Distraught, she felt rejected by everything, animate and inanimate – by the sky, by the trees, by other living things. And Martin supported her with the calm force of his personality. It was a strength that she needed. She had abandoned her university course before taking her degree. The goal for which she had struggled so long, with such passionate determination, had become a symbol of the social and intellectual bondage she was rejecting.

The couple arrived at Dover in the pouring rain, Maria unable to speak English, confronted by a cold distant land. Yet in her heart she felt that having given up everything, now she had found freedom. Martin's mother accepted her utterly and unquestioningly – her attitude being the simple and honest one that any choice of her son's must of necessity be the right one. 'All your troubles are past,' she wrote to Maria. 'Now your life lies only in front of you.'

No sooner were they landed than they went to the Registry Office and gave notice of their intended wedding. Then they settled in with Martin's parents. Maria went to work, in an electrical components factory, intent on earning enough money to pay those who had given her lodgings in Rome. It was hard work, monotonous and unexpectedly exhausting, but the money was amassed and repaid, and with it came a good working knowledge of English.

But then, after four months, Martin announced that the time had come to move again, this time in order to redeem a pledge to go and work for Danilo Dolci in Sicily. The fares were larger than they could reasonably hope to save, but this presented no hindrance to his resolve – they would simply go to Paris and hitch-hike. This time Maria had no desire at all to leave – she had found a home, and a sympathetic family in Martin's mother. Nevertheless, Martin willed it, so they returned.

Sicily, in July 1957, was desperately hot, and Dolci's work had still to achieve international glamour and with it international funds. The community, for such it was, lived in a bare house, with young men and women segregated by sex. In the daytime the men went with Danilo and tried practical ways of helping the critically poor Sicilians caught in the double claws of poverty and the Mafia. But it was largely a one-man show, depending on Dolci's riveting personality and increasingly on his access to political figures and to the world's press. Gradually Martin came to feel that he had nothing concrete to contribute to the work, that he was at best a supernumerary. Dolci's message was powerful but narrow, and by its very nature he seemed to be making practical rather than mystical progress – much of what Martin felt he was seeking was not to be found here. Maria, on the other hand, was by now working tremendously hard at the domestic side of the community, cooking and cleaning, regretting only that she had so little time to participate more fully in the spiritual side of the community. Martin's frustration, however, seemed to them both the deciding factor, and sadly they decided to return to London, where he would finally make up his mind what he wanted to do.

They took a small house in a terrace in Chiswick – smaller and darker than the large community building in the dazzling Sicilian countryside they had been accustomed to. Once more Maria went to work – but now she was pregnant. Martin too got a job – as a postman. It is a job, as Einstein once pronounced from experience, which gives one time to think. The time spent in reflection as he delivered the letters of the ratepayers of Chiswick bore fruit, albeit rather unexpectedly. One day Martin announced that he wanted to be a scientist. In practical terms it quite simply meant starting again from the bottom of the educational system, working his way up through 'O' and 'A' levels.

Martin left his job as soon as he was able, and started to study full-time – they would make do on Maria's wages until he was qualified. Maria too began to study once more and hoped that she would be able to devote herself to psychology full-time. But her everyday tasks were clearly too much, the bringing up of the children she was resolved to have would be too demanding, and bit by bit her studies took second place to the realities of life.

Martin and Maria's first child, a son, was born in 1958. For a name they chose Christian – for like Bunyan's character he was a steadfast sign that God was truly with them. But even in the midst of the disruptions caused by a small baby, the search for a 'way' continued. Once more they considered the idea of a community. There had been much which had suited them in the one they had lived in in Sicily, and now the isolation of the house in Chiswick seemed to grow more oppressive daily, the walls higher. True, Martin and Maria still found external contacts in work for Dolci's London committee, and their belief in pacifism had led them to the then-fashionable CND, but they wanted more. They reasoned that a community would be a living symbol of the pacifist way of life.

It was then that they heard of a community in Wales, in one of the hardest and least compromising parts of the country, where miners have suffered from strike and lockout for almost four generations. There has never even been a Conservative member on the town council and no election for Parliament has produced even the slightest sign of a serious Tory challenge. The inhabitants live in their back-to-back houses, which grow like the roots of a tree up to the very edge of the spoil heaps which the steel works have thrown up around the town.

In this part of Wales, the inhabitants are closed in upon themselves, proud of their socialist past, replete with the memory of strikes sustained, of blacklegs punished, of lockouts outfaced. And they are very Welsh – they sing together in great choirs, they talk passionately of rugby, and of the doings over in the other villages filled with kinsfolk bearing the same Welsh names. And they distrust outsiders.

In this forbidding place a community of social service had just been founded. Some Quakers owned a large, rather tumbledown house in the middle of the town, and they had given it to the community who were intent on serving the people of the town, as well as finding themselves through – or losing themselves in – the work and service. The leader of the community was a man named David, crippled after breaking his spine in a fall from the roof of a building project. By tremendous force of personality he had refused to be destroyed, and now here in the community he was living as full a life as possible, experiencing the outside world vicariously through the doings of his fellow members of the community. Other members worked on a pilot scheme making fibre-glass, or coped with the drunks, the down-and-outs, the beaten and ill-nourished children, the myriad social problems lurking behind the battered doors of the council houses.

Maria and Martin paid a visit to the community, to see if it would be a suitable place for them to go, taking with them their baby. They were welcomed, for they were the first married couple to wish to join, and their presence would be stabilising – furthermore new people are always welcome in the ingrown world of such institutions.

After experiencing the atmosphere, Martin made a characteristically direct decision. They would leave Chiswick in two weeks and go to live in Wales. It was impractical and inconvenient to leave everything at such short notice, but it *was* possible. 'Seek ye the Kingdom,' said Martin, 'and the rest shall be given to you.'

When they arrived they found that the community was in a period of crisis. There was only one woman member – an elderly school-teacher – and Maria was compelled once more to accept that she must undertake the cleaning and cooking. Martin began to work in the fibre-glass department, and gradually the community settled into an orderly pattern. Every morning there would be ten minutes of silent meeting; at the weekend the finances of the week would be discussed, the books balanced, and everybody would be given five shillings pocket money and could request the purchase of such articles of clothing from the common kitty as they needed. However spiritually refreshing this may have been, Maria found herself once more isolated from the very experience she and Martin had come to share: preparing the communal meals for upwards of a dozen members precluded her taking part in many of the most fruitful conversations. And when at weekends there were visitors, and music was sometimes played by mysterious and romantic Indians, as often as not Maria found herself at the sink.

And there was the problem of Christian. Intensely curious and interested in everything that went on around him, the child was not always wholly welcomed by some members of the community. Added to this the boy had the problem of adjusting himself to the fact that he now had to share his mother with a crowd of assorted adults. One day he stared fixedly at her and said: 'I want mother back' – and nothing would persuade him that everything was fundamentally unchanged.

To complicate matters still further, the community as a whole was in the grip of a deep malaise: some of the members had personal problems of their own and in reaction with each other they often generated an impossible atmosphere. In any community the temptation to back-bite and bitch behind each other's back is almost insurmountable, and friction and counter-friction are likely to build up till finally the community disintegrates.

Maria and Martin decided to return to Italy for a short visit because Maria's grandfather had died and she felt it her duty to support her grandmother. By now Adam, the second child, had been born and the two children went with them. At home in Perugia the atmosphere was better, since Martin had clearly proved that he was not a gold-digging adventurer. The family was stable, and there were children. But Alberto, Maria's brother, had made up his mind that his sister was returning to stay forever. He had even gone to the lengths of buying and equipping a fine new house in which she was going to live – fulfilling their childhood fantasy of having a home together. But there was nothing in Perugia for Martin to do, except sit around all day. Nobody seemed to have made any plans for him, his air of peaceful inactivity suggesting that he could easily be pushed to one side.

Further trouble resulted from something which seemed to Maria the great gain from this trip to Italy: the fact that they got to know the philosopher Aldo Capitini. His works were devoted to non-violence and a belief in 'the continuous living presence of all things – living and inanimate'. Maria drank in his mystical ideas avidly, but Capitini and his friends were deeply suspect with the bourgeoisie of Perugia, and were anathema to Maria's family. It was nothing short of a scandal that she and her husband should frequent these dangerous left-wing circles. Once more all the familiar family pressures were brought to bear on Maria and Martin, this time in an attempt to make them keep 'better company'.

Then one day, to the dismay of her brother, Maria announced that she was going to take her family and return to the community in Wales where she believed she, and above all Martin, were really needed. Alberto threw a tremendous scene and announced that if she left it would be for ever – that henceforward he had no sister.

As usual nothing would deflect them from their chosen course. In the spring of 1961 the family returned to Wales. Here they found the community no longer in a state of tension, but of collapse. Sadly, they realised that they could not continue living there, above all for the sake of the children, for Adam seemed lost and increasingly withdrawn in the confusing atmosphere of the community, and Christian clearly needed full-time care – something which the very problems associated with the community made almost impossible to achieve. They decided, therefore, with desperate reluctance, that the time had come to leave.

After a search a cottage was found, high on the spoil heaps behind the town. It was almost derelict and lay off the road about half a mile from the nearest house, four or five miles outside the town. Although the cottage was austere and isolated, the green grass clinging – albeit precariously – to the spoil heaps lent it an air of countryside. And the view over the town, with an ironmaster's folly of a castle rising beyond it, was disguised by distance into prettiness. They could have animals and flowers about them again, which they had missed badly in London and in the grimy centre of the Welsh town.

It was here that the family came in the autumn of 1964, leaving behind the painful memories of the community. And it was here that Maria and Martin began on what for them was the purpose of the whole quest: bringing up their children according to the 'process' which they had been developing and construing ever since they first met. The description of this process must be left for another chapter – the central chapter in this book: it is enough to say here that it would dictate an atmosphere and way of life which would make this cottage unlike any other, and would make tremendous demands on Maria.

For her the days ahead were to be ones of constant challenge, when every impulse would have to be carefully controlled and analysed, often in discussion with Martin when he returned home from the work he soon found as an assistant in a training college. Endlessly calm and patient, Martin could add wisdom and a deep natural purity to these discussions, helping Maria to carry on when her physical strength was at a low ebb. It was essential to 'the process' that she should give her time fully to the children, so she had to work out a regime by which she did her housework at night and managed with only four or five hours of sleep. On trying it out, she found that it worked, largely because the strain of the day had been so much lessened that it made up for the lack of the refreshment of sleep. Once she had established this, she was free to devote all the hours of daytime to the children and 'the process' of bringing them up.

CHAPTER THREE

MARTIN

Martin is in many ways the enigma of the family. Beside the active and articulate Maria he often seems to be intent on merging into the background, too ineffectual and too unassertive to play a significant part in the machinery of the family. But the longer one is in contact with the household, the more clearly one sees that this is a fundamental misconception. For the children, their father is as immediate and as available as their mother. Because he works during the day, Martin is unable to take a front-line part in the educational process his wife is following, but he has taken, as Maria is always intent on emphasising, an equally important part in formulating the process.

It is at home, with the children, that Martin most fully reveals himself. If Maria is an ideal mother, he is a perfect father. No sooner is he in the house than he and his children draw together, the youngsters showing absolutely none of the tension or caution that children often exhibit with their fathers.

Maria says of Martin that, unlike her, he is naturally good. His quality is one of stillness, repose and inner certainty. It is probably because the certainty is so strong that he feels little need to assert himself; and this certainty, so unwavering, might be criticised. To an outsider it might often seem that the family decisions which Martin has made and Maria has concurred with, such as uprooting them all at almost no notice to go to live in a community ill-suited to the bringing up of small children, showed scant respect for the convenience of others. But on the other hand there is great strength in such singleness of purpose. Most people let themselves be pushed by chance or other people's expectations into environments of which they make the best, rather than into those which meet their inner needs. Martin has persisted in attempting to find and at times create his own special environment.

Martin looks a typical Jewish immigrant from Eastern Europe, and is the son of an immigrant family. One glance at his hawknosed face, his shaggy, untrimmed beard and hair through which his earnest brown eyes peer questioningly, and one is reminded of a hundred haunting war-time photographs of refugees and concentration camps. His appearance, coupled with his remarkable closeness to his children, give him the unmistakable air of a Jewish father doting on and surrounded by a band of cherished offspring. But though he looks Jewish, the family character owes little to the popular traditional Jewish atmosphere. Maria is anything but possessive, the children anything but ambivalent in their attitude to their mother, and the fierce competitive ambition beloved of Jewish families is totally unknown to them. And nobody wants Ruth to marry a doctor. All that seems to remain of the Jewish background is Martin's overriding love and tenderness for the children.

His family came to England from Poland at the turn of the century. It was the time of the great Russian pogroms and everywhere Jews were leaving their homes and workshops in the ghettos of Eastern Europe and coming to find freedom and new homes in Western Europe. Many bundled up their scant possessions and came to England to set up workshops and businesses in the East End of London, simply putting down their packs as near to the ships that had carried them over as they could. Unable to speak the language of the country of their adoption, they formed once more into tight-knit communities, speaking Yiddish – the lingua franca of Jewry. Thus in London, if there were no walls to the ghettos, there were certainly linguistic and cultural barriers between the country of their adoption and the new Jewish arrivals.

Martin's grandfather, who had come from Poland and was a maker of walking-sticks, set up a workroom to follow his trade in the East End. At the beginning of the century it was a prosperous business, and by dint of tremendously hard work and self-sacrifice he succeeded in achieving a modest affluence, making canes and sticks for gentlemen of quality. His daughter, Martin's mother, married another Jew, and then went into business herself, running a small café in the suburbs of London. It was a typical, rather matriarchal Jewish home – but the children were happy and the mother, too, began to find her business modestly prosperous.

Then war broke out, and Nazi persecution seemed only a thin strip of water away. Whatever ancestors the family may have left behind in Poland were forgotten, whatever relatives they may have had were probably swept away in the holocaust that followed Hitler's invasion of Poland.

The war also brought a trauma for Martin and for his elder brother, who is now a post office engineer; for, like the displaced Jews of Europe, they were to be denied a stable place in which to pass their childhood. Fearful of the blitz on London, mindful of the fate of the Jews in occupied Europe, their mother allowed her sons to be evacuated out of London to a place of greater safety in Dorset. Evacuee children were a familiar sight at the beginning of the war, standing in disconsolate groups at railway stations, their names on luggage labels round their necks, waiting to be shipped willy-nilly to they knew not where.

Martin and his brother were lucky in that they were destined for a respectable middle-class home in a sleepy country town, but nevertheless the two small boys were deeply and desperately unsettled by reason of their Jewishness and all that it meant, as well as by the upset and disruption of evacuation.

Their new home, near the southern port of Poole, was pleasant; the childless middle-aged couple who had taken them in was kind, if a little ignorant of the ways of the children. They accepted the two dark, beady-eyed children whole-heartedly into their home, and the boys went to the local school. It was a country school, the children speaking with the raw open vowel sounds of Dorset and tightly clannish in their ways. They looked askance at the eccentric strangers, and the bolder ones whispered the charged word 'Jew' in safely remote corners, out of earshot of the teachers. Martin was unhappy, though his older brother proved resilient and fitted in better.

When at the age of eleven the time came for them to go on to their secondary schools, Martin had done less well and found he was to go to the lower secondary modern, while his brother passed into the grammar school. At their adopted home things were calm, but neither of the children was entirely happy, and predictably they grew close together. In the evenings their adopted father would give vent to tirades against the Jews, responsible according to him for all the multiple ills that afflicted the world. He was in many ways a generous and warm man; he was only giving tongue to an unthinking prejudice, and had forgotten perhaps – if indeed he had ever known – that the two East End children he was harbouring in his home were Jews. But for the boys it was intensely embarrassing. Should they allow him to rant on, or should they interrupt and remind him of their race? It was a social problem which they never succeeded in resolving before – the war over – they returned with relief and joy to their mother and the café she still ran in West London, undisrupted by the blitz or by rationing.

Martin and his brother were overjoyed to be once more in familiar surroundings, and soon settled down to the everyday routine of home life. At his new London school Martin began to do better – now more settled, he was able to devote fresh time and energy to his work. He attended the local grammar school, one of the highly efficient suburban London schools which yearly turn out scores of school-teachers and pharmacists, solicitors, clerks and house-agents. His progress, not surprisingly since he had under-

37

gone so interrupted an education during the previous five years, was unspectacular, but it was more than adequate. By the time he was eighteen and in the sixth form he was numbered by his teachers among those boys who would proceed, worthily, if not outstandingly, to university. He was to study modern languages.

Now for the first time Martin asserted a decisive independence of will. He was not, he announced, going to university. He could see no purpose in it. In vain his teachers pointed out the academic and social advantages, and his mother protested that everybody had always believed he would carry on with his studies. But then as now, once his mind was made up Martin was immovable. Furthermore he revealed a second surprising piece of intelligence – not only had he decided on the futility of higher education, but he had no other career in mind. Unlike his schoolfellows, all of whom were only too conscious of the places they would occupy in the system, Martin proposed to opt out.

It was long before the days of the hippy and the dropout, and Martin's intention constituted a considerably surprising gesture. To his family he simply let it be known that since he had yet to decide what he wanted to do in life, he proposed to drift until he had had good time to make up his mind. Although dismayed, his mother knew him too well to protest, and Martin set off to France, officially to practise his French and unofficially, in due course, to decide what he would do with his life.

Like the hippies of today he drifted aimlessly about Europe, finally ending up on a vineyard in the South West of France, helping with the harvest. Gentle, already slightly stooping, but with an ineffable air of knowing his own mind, he was fatally attractive to the local girls, who saw in him a need for mothering coupled with a deep inner strength which each felt that she alone could channel and bring forth. He developed an intense emotional relationship with a French girl, her parents reacted with predictable outrage at the foreign Jewish seducer, and after suitable gestures his residence permit was withdrawn. Willy-nilly Martin found himself in Italy.

He took up residence in Milan, a centre for left-wing students and social experiments. There he joined an early commune, and supported himself by giving English lessons. The community, however, was something of a failure, as often seems to happen with such experiments, and he moved, disillusioned, to Rome. Here he hovered on the edge of the University, going to lectures and joining student activities, but still giving English lessons for a living. Intense, shabby, poor, he fitted easily into the tolerant, eclectic atmosphere of Rome University. Already addicted to good causes, keenly aware of a sharp, typically Jewish social conscience, Martin spent his spare time working for the embryonic and politically charged cause of the Sicilian reformer, Danilo Dolci. Many of his friends were involved with writing pamphlets, duplicating them, distributing them, and between times talking about how best the world could be improved.

In the midst of this hectic activity he met Maria, then an intensely shy girl staying with the Spanish nuns, and passing all her spare time in the study of Greek philology in the library. Very soon a rapport built up between them. They passed hours talking about life, about religion, about society, and about the children they would have and how they must bring them up in a way which would avoid the traumas of their own childhoods and allow them a full and free development. Both of them were deeply serious, both were as good listeners as they were talkers. And above all both of them had an intense feeling of apartness, of not fitting in. Between them, as the months developed, was born a great feeling of understanding, and then of love.

Martin had given way to the violent family reaction inspired by his relationship with the French girl, but this time his certainty was greater and the girl was stronger. The two of them were ideally suited to each other, and although the determined hostility of Maria's family caused her great distress, it never succeeded in making him waver. Their notion that they could drive him off by depriving Maria of her money was so absurdly far from the truth of his nature that it meant nothing to him. Martin at last believed that he knew what he wanted to do. He would start again at the bottom of the educational tree and become a scientist. With steady determination he began again on his 'O' levels, and worked his way slowly and with considerable difficulty upwards. Often he failed exams, but he always tried again until he achieved them. Obviously, this type of activity placed additional strains on Maria. Often she had periods when she had to be the breadwinner, as often Martin worked at home at his books, making it difficult for her to carry on everyday housework.

Such rejection of conventional marital responsibilities may seem selfish, but it was simply part of Martin's resolve that nothing should deflect him from what he knew to be right. Furthermore, the division inside a family between 'them' and 'me' simply never occurred to him. For these two people man and wife make up a single unit, each taking up the burden at need, and without question. It is part of the feeling of strength they generate.

Today such a union of two 'Nowhere People' would seem less exceptional than it did fifteen years ago, but would be no more likely to succeed in its own terms. Whatever the powerful emotional chemistry which drew two such seemingly lost people together, the genetic mixture was to prove as exceptionally powerful. From a combination of Maria's resolve and power, and Martin's certainty and belief in the strength of absolutes, was to grow an exceptional educational process and a family of exceptional children.

CHAPTER FOUR

THE PROCESS

'The process' – and for Maria and Martin it is truly a process, a continuing living thing – is compounded of 'love'. It is easy, when one is surrounded by hardened and exploited uses of the word, to find it embarrassing when it is written on a page, but Maria believes fully and completely in the power of love, as simply as the medieval mystics or St Theresa of Avila did, although for her and Martin it is not 'love' in the strictly Christian context, but rather in the context of a social world, devoid of tensions and stresses of social and anti-social conflict.

From her earliest days at Rome University, Maria had resolved that when she had children they would be brought up free from all pressures which might lead to undesirable social behaviour – violence, hatred, jealousy or spite. Her intention was not to bring them up so isolated from society that they would, when adult, find themselves unable to adjust to the 'wickedness of the world'. Her goal was simple: that her children should be themselves so 'social' that they would be free of all anti-social impulses. Her method of achieving this would be love. The setting: an environment which could be totally controlled until the children were able to take part in the outside world. While most people would write this off as naive and impractical dreaming, to her and Martin it was something which they could and must achieve.

While she was still living in London, Maria had taken a course in Montessori teaching. Now, in the Welsh cottage, using and adapting these methods, she set about providing

41

for the formal educational needs of the children, buying or simply inventing the desired apparatus. Above all, she reasoned, they needed full-time total care and attention divorced from the time-wasting and distractions of the classroom. Central to her process was the belief that in the development of the mind there are certain periods of sensitivity when briefly, sometimes only for a few hours, the mind is prepared to accept and digest a new piece of information; when, as it were, the doors of perception are open. When the child achieves this state, when the door into its mind is open, if nobody is prepared to help or is ready to listen, the door may swing shut, possibly never to open again. And, as a side effect, general development and the capacity to make social adjustments will be damaged. But if someone is present, ready and prepared at all times, then the moments will be caught, the step made. Then the process of learning will be easy and free from strain.

All that is required is that the mother or teacher should be constantly available and vigilant. If the cup of learning – in the broadest sense – is constantly proffered when the child is thirsty, it will drink. Then there will be no struggle to compel reluctant children to concentrate on subjects to which they were uniquely receptive weeks or even hours before. Following this theory, ever-present in an environment which eliminated distractions, Maria watched and helped through the times when the children learnt. Sometimes all went smoothly; sometimes the children seemed to get themselves into impasses from which they had difficulty in extricating themselves. With total patience and serenity she persevered, and was rewarded when they escaped with a startling lateral bound. Above all, she learnt, she must not be attached to results, or put any pressure on the children however disappointed or exhausted she might feel herself. It is of no consequence if children can or cannot read at a certain age, do long division or whatever at a certain age. Freedom from pressure is far more important than laboured and stressful progress. Constantly Maria reminded herself of this, looked to the horizon and persevered.

And now there was another lesson. If there was to be equal pleasure in learning and play, then the division between the two must not be distinct. Increasingly in the Welsh cottage there was less formal differentiation between 'school hours' and 'home hours'. All day long Maria would sit with the children, playing with them, discussing things in a low unemotional voice. The Montessori teaching aids Martin had made for them intermingled with the toys and paints with which they diverted themselves. And to the children there was no difference between the two. Whether they wanted to play or to paint, their mother aided them. Whether they wanted to play mathematics or play reading, she was equally available. And her constant physical presence, uninterrupted by household chores or outside distractions, meant that she was able to grasp the slightest sensitive period at whatever time it manifested itself. Serene herself, knowing now that she was doing something for which her previous reading and spiritual searching had qualified her uniquely, Maria transferred her serenity to the children. At best progress was spectacular, at worst, constant.

Maria now began to face the second real task of an educator, that of finding for each child an outlet, a uniquely suitable method of self-expression. Adam, often silent and withdrawn, was led gently to music. His interest was first kindled by a toy piano he set his heart on in Woolworths in the local market town. Maria bought it for his birthday. Later an elderly second-hand piano, acquired for twelve pounds, was brought up the hill. Not only was it a new game – it was a way to self-discovery for the frail boy. Maria, unable to read music herself, set about bringing Adam to a personal fruition through the piano. A form of play was devised – and Maria herself mastered the simple principles of musical notation.

She was to be Mummy Tortoise, he, Adam Hare. The hare was to lead the way, effortlessly and brilliantly; the tortoise was to follow on behind. Initially, the boy found progress difficult, his failures at drawing the sounds in his head out of the piano before him were terribly frustrating. But soon progress became faster, fulfilment nearer, as the hare far outstripped the tortoise. In this process the role of the mother-teacher proved wholly successful. Progress was made only after the more carefully nurtured and controlled beginnings. No pressure was applied, always it was the child who led, not the teacher. Confidence was gained, the right course seeming to present itself as if by its own volition. In a schoolroom context such a thing would have proved difficult, if not impossible to organise, and above all Adam could scarcely have been kept free from pressure either of competition with other children, or simply of competition for the limited time of the teacher. As it was, he was free to master the first steps with extreme caution, and was equally free of any hindrance when it came to ascending further up the ladder to what was later to become a total involvement with music.

Those who have not tried to educate children at home foresee in such a scheme difficulties both of discipline in its narrowest sense, and in the dual role of the mother-teacher. It is perhaps because with their children the worlds of 'school' and 'home' are so divergent as to be irreconcilable. It is also sadly true that, fond as they may be, some parents have an underlying uneasiness in the presence of their children, a reluctance to treat them on the basis of equality, and this uneasiness would make a protracted contact in a learning context hard to accept. Maria found no such difficulty, and since the children perceived no sense of uneasiness in her, they too accepted totally that their mother and teacher are one. It is a case of action being the sole eroder of barriers, or trial being the only way of striking the proper sort of relationship with one's own children.

But the paramount difficulty, in the eyes of conventional

parents, is the one of discipline. To the old-fashioned discipline is an abstract virtue, like chastity or patriotism, compounded of fear of retribution and respect for the dignity of self-restraint. Since instilling such a virtue into children is less agreeable than indulging them, the modern parent seizes on his natural desire that his children should not be afraid of him as an excuse for off-loading the painful and unpleasant task of ticking-off, or even chastising, the children, onto somebody else who is paid for the job. That the whole weight of this process should fall on the home is inconceivable – and since undisciplined, or ill-disciplined children are known to be uncontrollably wild, spared rods and spoiled children are both best kept at arms length. All this, of course, postulates a very narrow view of discipline, and one which, in the minds of many parents, is confused with the idea of corporal punishment, or at least physical restraint.

Such attitudes have absolutely no place in Maria and Martin's scheme of things. They are totally committed to a non-violent ethic, and there could be no question of violence, or even near-violence, in relation to children. Smacking, Maria reasons, only represents a release of pressure for the mother and is at best a signal for the child to desist from an action not because it is 'wrong' – a concept little children are incapable of comprehending – but because it will inexplicably bring down on it unpleasant and deeply disturbing sanctions. None of Maria's children has ever been even scolded, let alone struck or smacked. She apologises instantly to them if she has spoken impatiently to them under stress. And this lack of violence seems to be reflected in the children, who feel no need of any form of cathartic release from violence around them.

Their games are devoid of guns, or sudden death, or even any sort of wrestling or pushing. When there is violence in them it is in fantasies of confounding mythical figures, such as Paul's Badcat, an evil manifestation. Even in these games, Badcat is discountenanced rather than destroyed. In play, as in anger, it is inconceivable that one child should hit another – it simply does not happen. In an environment free from violent sanctions the children seem free themselves from any desire to hurt each other. In this Martin and Maria seem to have been totally successful – non-violence in their upbringing seems to have freed the children from the sin of Cain. Adam, bullied at school, would say: 'You can make holes in me, but you can't really hurt me,' and was not simply parrotting something he had been taught to say at home, but was expressing what for him was a self-evident truth. Nobody at Christian's school can remember him ever resorting to any kind of violence to whatever end. He used only his tongue to protect himself from his school-fellows. And even this worried his parents – he was hurting people in speech, which was spiritually painful. For them this might represent a failure in Christian, and thus in the process.

However, this is only to touch on the more 'negative' side of discipline. Maria tries to look at its positive, constructive side. The children accept that certain rules of conduct *are* necessary, and that only by following them can they hope to achieve anything. Even when they were very small they seemed to perceive that quarrelling is sterile, routine constructive. Finding, as they all do, real pleasure in mastering mathematics, in music, in painting or model-making, they consider a measure of organisation and self-discipline as part of the fascination of mastering new skills. Maria, aware that disciplines imparted in this way are stronger than those reinforced only by sanctions, tried always when explaining a play process or an intellectual hurdle to inject the required discipline into the learning process at the outset. It saved, she found, the need for conventional discipline and sanctions later on.

To bring up children as Maria and Martin have done involves more than simply a physically pure environment, or even genetically gifted raw material. It demands first and foremost a total and long-lasting dedication to the children, an almost mystical dedication of their mother's life to their upbringing. Indeed it is this vital dedication which many people find hardest to adjust to when confronted by Maria's way of bringing up children. It is quite simply not natural, they protest, to expect mothers to lose themselves so completely in their children.

In a sense mothers who feel this are right in the purely social context. In giving themselves totally to their children, they would inevitably sacrifice a certain amount of self, and, if their husbands were not as dedicated as Martin has proved to be, they would also risk some sort of damage to their marriage. But Maria has no such problems, and can rely on Martin's support and participation. For her the essence of love is strengthened by sacrifice, and she points out that it only takes about ten years to bring a child through its most critical stages. The sacrifice may be total – but it isn't permanent. Mothers, Maria believes, should be prepared to forego ambition, even comfort, during this time. When the children have formed, time enough to pick up the threads of an outside life again.

In essence, one must begin by giving oneself. Try for the Kingdom, as Martin believes, and the rest will be given to you. Given a total dedication, the tasks that a mother has to undertake are compounded simply of patience and more patience, of watching and waiting.

All mothers, of course, dedicate themselves to their children in the sense that they are perforce deeply involved in them – even an outside job cannot wholly prevent it. And most mothers spend almost all their time with their babies, especially when they are young. But this is not really enough – mere presence is no substitute for what Maria would call 'togetherness': the act of losing oneself in one's baby. Maria has always tried, as it were, to immerse herself in each child, to identify completely with its problems and difficulties, and to wrestle with these problems as though they were her own.

As each child was born, both parents tried thus to merge

themselves into 'the new life that was entrusted to them'. It was almost as though at the traumatic moment of birth, when perception is so heightened, everything went into the melting pot, leaving Maria ready to cope afresh with everything, wholly re-dedicated to the new baby.

She claims that far from sacrificing herself, she has turned the inevitable preoccupation with her children to a great strength of peace and happiness – that through experiencing 'togetherness' she has herself become emotionally richer. Those who know her would feel that she exists sometimes under tremendous strain, but that she has also an inner serenity that comes of peace of mind. Sacrifices she may have made, but to her they have only been the extensions of an appointed task, with the attendant compensations of having fulfilled that task well.

In the first seven years of a child's growth, as defined in Piaget,* the child is still having difficulty in expressing his thoughts through the use of language. It is a time for the mother to help in fostering early sensory perception, in encouraging the child to explore the world around it by making use of its senses of touch, of colour, of smell. Christian, before he could speak, was able to differentiate between colours, and for hours his mother would aid him as he sorted crates of toy milk bottles from one colour to another. Patience and constant presence are vital. Experiments may need to be repeated scores of times before they are successful.

As the baby ceases passively to accept the universe about it, and begins to make its first tentative explorations of the outside world, the mother finds that she has taken on the role of educator quite as fully as if she were sitting in a classroom trying to teach a group of recalcitrant sixth formers.

* The Swiss child psychologist Jean Piaget (born 1896) has identified and codified the various stages of infant growth and evolution. His numerous books, based on nearly fifty years research at Geneva University, are indispensable to understanding child development.

Her first rule must be that she should be positive and not negative in the pattern of her lessons – above all she must never restrict her child's curiosity by simply forbidding a course of action. Children will often wish to repeat a single act – such as throwing a toy out of the cot – seemingly endlessly. In essence it is exploring space and distance by judging the time the toy takes to fall to the ground, the sound it makes and so forth. Maria is prepared to allow the baby to repeat the act until it desists – if necessary for days at a time. Nor is she squeamish about excreta or other bodily functions, or nervously hypercautious about potentially damaging elements in the immediate environment. When the children decided to play 'potty bombs' she allowed this, as she had allowed all other exploratory play. For an afternoon they played messily in the bathroom. When their curiosity was slaked and the taboo seemed expurgated she cleaned up, and after this experience the children never wished to repeat the game or even referred to it. It needed considerable strength of conviction, but the effect justified overcoming what in effect might seem to be the adult's rather than the children's excreta taboo.

Doors onto the mind can be shut as easily and as permanently at the outset as in the later stages of a child's development. Infinite patience is always essential. An over-strained mother may well want to slap a child and take away something potentially dangerous or simply noisy. While this may release the mother's tensions, it serves only to frighten the child and inhibit an experiment about the nature of his surroundings which the child may not feel able to commence again for several days. A hundred such reverses are bound to have an appreciable hindering effect on a child's development.

The preparation of the environment and the control of it are equally important. Maria attached the greatest possible importance to it, and constructed for herself in effect an ideal controlled environment, sacrificing almost everything to obtain it. For she believes that a prepared environment is as important for a child as the special food a baby needs for its growth. On the face of it, the preparation of an environment sufficiently pure and remote to be free from distractions, but sufficiently attached to society not to impose intolerable strains of loneliness or isolation on the mother, is an almost impossibly difficult task. But only in peace, away from every form of irrelevant stimulation or outside pressure, can the child develop harmoniously with all its evolutionary processes developing at the same rate, avoiding schizoid or unbalanced characteristics in later life. In total peace a child will not feel threatened, either by spoken or unspoken pressures. He will not be even unconsciously concerned with preserving himself or keeping his emotional balance. It is only in this peace, Maria feels, that children will be free to listen and to explore – and no sacrifice is too great to achieve it. To follow 'the process', first an environment *must* be found and prepared. Materially difficult though it may be, without this framework nothing is possible. For the prepared environment, by avoiding all sorts of conflicts, will make it possible to open all the doors of perception, and allow development and curiosity to go hand in hand.

Once her prepared environment had been achieved in the home on the hill, Maria embarked on a carefully prepared plan of activities, embracing rituals and learning games as well as specifically developed apparatus. The latter, however, proved not to be as useful as she and Martin had anticipated and was often changed or discarded altogether – though the Montessori-based toys were often the best and most enduring. Part of this failure was because Maria found in herself a tendency to become too attached to the apparatus or toys themselves, and to the logical and time-filling patterns they provided for her, which could blind her to the obvious fact that the children had played out these particular aids. Too often Maria found that materials designed by people not directly concerned in an individual parent-child relationship turned out, when judged in the light of a carefully prepared environment, to be designed not for any particular purpose beyond diverting the child and killing time. Sometimes, it is true, a specific toy presented a challenge, but as often another was discarded – a living example of the old adage that the best toy is a simple one. It was not complex adult-inspired toys, but pens and paper, raffia and small home-made looms which provided Maria and her children with endless hours exploring their senses and reflexes, and later with improvised scientific experiments and games of imagination.

Simply finding and providing a prepared environment is not enough. However great the effort of achieving this, it must not be allowed to exhaust energy. The composition and character of any environment is inevitably affected by the different phases of the development of the child for whom it was prepared, both physically and intellectually. Maria found that it is essential that the environment should develop as the child develops, otherwise tensions seemed to appear within it which inhibited any proper reciprocal relationship between her and her baby.

For instance, at an early stage, the more the mother plays with her child, and the more the conversation is pitched above the child's present capability and not below it, the quicker the child's development will be. Maria found that when Christian was playing with shaped wooden blocks, fitting into the slotted lid of a box, it both helped his physical co-ordination and stimulated his curiosity in the physical nature of the objects themselves. And there was an unexpected and important breakthrough on the developmental front: through this game Christian became more aware of the fallacies inherent in his egocentric view of life. By refusing to obey his whim, the recalcitrant blocks showed him that their physical properties were not subject to his will – that they had as it were a life independent of him. Maria immediately seized on the opportunity presented by Christian's apparent awareness of the physical properties of this game to introduce comparative terminology.

The blocks were taller, thinner, shorter, thicker and so forth. Now Christian knew he could name their properties and was able to use words to set them in order. Thus, this game which diverted him for many hours, contained lessons in physical co-ordination, in the nature of inanimate physical objects in the outside world, and in vocabulary.

Similarly the prepared environment allowed Maria freedom to permit experiments which most mothers would find intolerable in an average home. Thus, by the time he was a year old, Christian was experimenting with water toys, pouring liquid into containers of different sizes and shapes, working out the volumes needed to fill one bottle from another. It was perforce a very messy game, sometimes the table or floor would be swimming in water, but Maria never forbade him, never did anything to curtail his experiments, till he was satisfied that he had discovered what his curiosity demanded and stopped them of his own accord.

Maria watched over these experiments, taking the greatest care not to introduce new ones to Christian until he seemed to have absorbed the lessons of the previous ones: until, in fact, she judged the doors of perception were open once more and he was ready to receive new information. It is not always easy, of course, to know when that point is reached. It is possible for a game which no longer contains any new information to become a ritual which the child repeats again and again from habit rather than interest. Sometimes it is only because the child starts to show generalised frustration that a mother can tell that he is ready once more to assimilate fresh information. For example, at the age of four and a half Paul seemed to lose interest in painting, which he had enjoyed enormously until then, and for the first time he began to become irritated at the slightest frustration, while his all-round progress seemed to be slowing down. Maria and Martin, after careful deliberation on what solution the process demanded, decided that their son required a chance to come to grips with creating more impressive and desirable structures than were possible with toy bricks, and with the problems of co-ordination and design presented by full-scale craftsmanship. They saved up and bought Paul a work bench, complete with real adult-sized tools. Almost instantly it was apparent that they had lighted on the right decision – he became fascinated with the possibilities of carpentry and spent hours with his father on elementary woodwork. At the same time he began to take his own pleasure in painting again. The block from which he had been suffering had been broken down.

This need to avoid frustration and dead-ends is doubly important with small babies, since they take longer to assimilate information from an often repeated physical act, and the whole time scale is infinitely more difficult to judge. Sometimes babies will wish to repeat an act relentlessly until their mother finds her patience under the gravest possible strain. It is a situation in which there are no short cuts, in which only patience will result in the child uncovering the knowledge it wants. Above all, the mother must not lose her temper or stop the child from repeating an exploratory act as long as it needs to, even if it makes no sense to an adult.

For instance, once Maria decided that instead of allowing Paul to drop his rattle literally hundreds of times out of his cot, she would tie it onto a piece of string, partly so that he could learn to haul it up again, and partly so that she would not need to wash it every time it landed on the floor. The child howled. Unless the rattle fell to the floor, making a noise, the experiment simply didn't seem worthwhile to him. It was only when Maria recommenced the dropping-washing-dropping-again cycle that Paul was able to satisfy his curiosity by gathering all the physical information available in his exploratory game.

Similarly, in an attempt to keep Christian occupied when he was eight months old, Maria hung pieces of coloured cloth from the ceiling above his cot. At first he gazed enraptured at them, but then she found that he became bored unless elastic was used to attach them to the ceiling.

He would then tug at them and muscular co-ordination became part of the lesson he was learning. With string he could only handle them, learning the simple lesson of their texture, and his attention soon wandered to something else.

The prepared environment is equally important in the next stage, when the baby has first learned to talk. Then there will be scope for an endless exchange of words between the mother and child, but if this is allowed to happen in an entirely random fashion, a lot of the child's creative energies will be expended in pursuing unnecessary diversion of vocabulary and meaning. To avoid this Maria set about deliberately classifying the vocabulary she felt the children should learn, trying to make use of their exploratory instincts, hoping to harness their innate sense of orderliness to the development of their vocabulary. After she and Martin had discussed it, the father put shelves around the babies' cots. On these Maria arranged all the child's possessions in a rigid order – soap, baby powder, nappies, toys, clothes and so on, always in exactly the same place, and every time she or Martin picked something up they would name it out loud before replacing it in the same spot. Soon Christian was repeating the words after, and then before, his parents. When he had become thoroughly familiar with the names of all the objects surrounding him, Maria would put them all in a bag and let him select one by touch. Inevitably Christian would know both its name and its place on the shelves which surrounded his cot.

In this prepared environment, learning to write and read follows the same exploratory pattern. Writing happens before reading, while reading follows a similar pattern to the development of speech – a question of collecting a vocabulary of understood words. Writing, on the other hand, needs both physical control of the movements and an ability to co-ordinate brain and written information on the page. When Christian was two and a half he began to become interested in writing, and Maria and Martin accordingly did their best to prepare for what they believed was the next phase in his development. Between them they set about the laborious process of making a set of letters out of sandpaper so as to be able to introduce the letters of the alphabet to Christian when the time came – the standard Montessori method. They thought he would be ready some time around his third birthday, and planned to have the alphabet waiting for the moment when his mind seemed uniquely receptive to this information. Then one day, when Christian was still only two and a half, he saw a set of plastic capital letters in a shop window and immediately announced that he wanted them. He proved so determined that Maria emptied out her purse, scraped up the price and bought them then and there. Already at two and a half Christian could memorize photographically the actual characters composing the words of almost everything that was read to him, so that no sooner was he home with the plastic letters than he started making up complete words with them. Within an hour, to his parents' astonishment, he had made the words 'train' and 'engine'. Unfortunately Martin had not yet completed the lower-case sandpaper letters, and as a result Christian started to work with the capitals, becoming daily more absorbed with the word games that Maria invented and played with him. This lack of lower-case had a side effect – for until Christian was nearly six he worked with more ease and fluency in capitals than with small letters.

Although she soon sensed Christian's natural propensity for mathematics, Maria tried not to introduce him to numbers as though they were a distinct and separate discipline. Martin made for her a set of number rods in which sections were painted in two distinctive colours. Thus the child first meets differing quantities as if they are objects with a physical reality of their own, and adding and subtracting, simple multiplication and division can be achieved without any inhibiting complex explanation of numerical theory. Armed with these aids, Christian bounded through the early stages of mathematics.

Children are capable of quite difficult mathematical thought. For instance, at four Paul was able to understand the concept of negative numbers, simply because Maria had been on hand to see that all his previous questions were promptly answered and the appropriate piece of equipment was provided as soon as the doors of perception opened. One day he simply asked 'What happens if you take away ten from nine?' Most parents would have answered 'You can't,' believing any other answer to be too difficult for a four-year-old to understand. This would have closed the door that was open, and when he was finally confronted by the concept of negative numbers at his secondary school, he would have found difficulty in believing that there was any rational answer to the question. Paul asked the question as he was walking through the Welsh countryside, apparently quite casually. Maria hurried him home, drew him a chart showing zero in the centre, positive numbers on one side, negative numbers on the other. A complication arose – Paul, at four, had already experimented with fractions. Now he asked where these lay. Was it, he asked, between one and two, and if so was there another way of writing them with a single number? Maria, seeing that the doors of perception were open, simply explained about decimals and then drew another chart, very large, expressing negative numbers but using the decimal principle for the intermediate quantities. From this sudden curiosity, instantly answered, Paul gathered a different conception of the true balance of zero which up till then had simply meant for him 'nothing'. He was radiant. For him this was a very wonderful gain, and one which he came to share with me next morning when he woke me up to have a discussion about negative quantities.

As a child gets older, he becomes increasingly capable of playing *with* other children, rather than playing alongside them, and the imaginative games which result often act as a safety valve. Untroubled by any fear of their own violence, Maria's children often seemed to be playing with remarkable lack of inhibition. She always takes the greatest care not to become concerned or frightened by the intensity of the emotions they seem to be playing out. Paul and Christian when playing together, as they often do, seem to select ordinary everyday objects – such as gear wheels or electrical components – and by giving them special properties transform them into objects in a fantastic world capable of unlimited acts. Evil forces appear in these games, but they are always overcome – by superior powers of light rather than by retributive violence – and the children return radiant and unconcerned to their usual pursuits.

There is bound to come a time when the child begins to wish to experiment with life outside the prepared environment. Maria is quite clear in her appreciation of this fact. When the children are no longer at the stage of their development when they are perforce wrapped up in themselves, they will want to plunge into the environment of the outside world. Then, she knows, much of what she has so laboriously prepared will become obsolete, for the prepared environment is only a staging post. When the children want to move out, Maria will have to be terribly strong, and unattached to the substance of their childhood and what she has built up. 'Outside' will seem almost impossibly threatening; the social values of society totally at odds with everything she and Martin have worked for.

To a certain extent the charmed circle of the prepared environment has already been broken by the older children. When Christian and Adam were ready to try their first tentative footsteps in the outside environment of their first formal school, Maria and Martin carefully reined back their very natural feeling they had at all costs to keep their children in the more pure environment that they had so laboriously built around them. Instead, they tried to start a dialogue with the world to which Christian and Adam would have to adjust. Maria and Martin were quite realistic enough to see that they had hopelessly cut themselves off from much of what passes as everyday life, nor did they nurse any real hope that the unsympathetic world of the Welsh schoolroom could be altered. They had to attempt to show the children that their parents too were concerned in the joys and dilemmas of the world outside, and would share with them in the crises and rewards that might arise.

They expected difficulties. For instance, because dialogue between siblings in a prepared environment is totally free-flowing, it is often difficult for them to understand that free dialogue does not exist outside. But even so there are compensations, for when children are willing of their own volition to operate in the ordinary world outside their prepared environment they will take with them the language and the awareness of the enclosed community they came from. Because of their almost unique awareness of other people, Christian and Adam were, Maria believes, able to adjust continuously and successfully to ordinary everyday standards.

Children brought up as hers have been will often have learnt already many of the major lessons of life. Thus Maria's children, she believes, have already learned to be truly responsible, not because they are afraid of punishment, but because they are able truly to put themselves in the place of others – and indeed this is something which is an everyday act in the prepared environment in which they began their development.

She also feels that Christian and Adam are coming up to the age of adolescence both more liberated from prejudice and more capable of abstract thought than almost any children of their own age. For Maria sees the true test of the prepared environment coming at the moment when the children step outside it. She believes that her children, far from cowering in the emotional peace and security she has built around them, are better prepared to face the vicissitudes of the outside world now that they are increasingly forced to come into contact with it.

At present it seems as if she is right. On the Welsh hillside, cut off from the town, there is an undeniable feeling of serenity. Apart from the offchance of a visit by 'a person from Porlock' there is hardly any distraction. Indeed, during the daytime Maria even asks that she should not be telephoned, so that nothing will disturb her when she is occupied with Paul and his 'process'. This freedom from distraction allows for such extra elements as letting the child make controlled mistakes – a Montessori concept – and gives her the uninterrupted time necessary to help the child develop as wide and rich a vocabulary of words as possible. It is through this mastering of the basic tool of communication that the child gains the understanding which allows him to progress quickly and easily later on. His mistakes should not be corrected too fussily. The child should simply be engaged in constant conversation as rich and adult in its use of words as seems suitable. It is never a good idea to talk down to children. As every mother who has brought up children knows, the best children's books are those which are adult in their language, like the Beatrix Potter stories. The same is true of conversation. 'Baby talk' is as bad a medium of communication as Hottentot.

The mother must also be aware of the importance of avoiding any kind of conflict, or charged relationship with objects, animate and inanimate, or people. Any such disturbance will be transmitted to the child and will delay the process. It is for this reason that Maria has tried to keep violence, frustration and pent-up emotions out of her life as far as possible. Serenity is vitally important to the child's progress. Children detect upset in the surrounding atmosphere very readily, even if it isn't openly expressed by their parents. Recently Maria was staying with her family as guests in a friend's house. Just before the time came for them to leave, she asked the children not to go to the fridge, for fear there would be accidents. Nevertheless, their desire to experiment was too strong, and a cup full of ice cubes was produced as a play-object. Maria, under the pressures of the social situation, whipped them away.

'You've *destroyed* them,' Paul cried. 'Why have you *destroyed* them?'

For Maria this seemingly trivial incident represented a failure – something to be recorded and avoided in future – because she had subjected Paul to an uncharacteristic and unsettling manifestation of her own disquiet.

Usually she reacts to situations which other mothers would hardly consider as impinging on the area of child-rearing, by ignoring the pressures and conventions of every-day life to an almost comical extent. For example, if Paul, on the way to the bus stop, becomes absorbed with the goods on display in the greengrocers, she will refuse to hurry him up until she is satisfied that what seems to her his very reasonable interest has been slaked. The fact of missing the bus is a very minor consideration. But such an attitude has its own rewards. If catching the bus is really important – if it is the last one, or one which is being met – Paul, without any loss of serenity, can be persuaded to come on. Outsiders often find such spectacles amusing, since children of four and a half are seldom allowed to engage in logical arguments with their parents before deciding to do what they are asked.

But it is not a simple question of discipline – it is also one of heightening the essential reciprocal relationship between mother and child. By exploring together the pros and cons of even a simple and seemingly self-evident decision such as whether or not to stop looking at apples and catch a bus, Paul is being helped to become more aware of the reality of other people, of their motives and emotions. By being drawn, through his awareness of his mother, away from his egocentric obsessions he is being helped, in Maria's view, through a vital stage in his development.

This is also why Maria places great store by the practice of giving presents within a family – the creative exchange of gifts, as she calls it. At moments of strain or of happiness Maria gives the children small home-made tokens such as a painting or a piece of needlework. And the children, too, will give small things to each other, not only to mark a special stress or occasion, but also as a sign of involvement in the crisis. It helps, Maria believes, to cement a 'togetherness' in the family, to heighten a belief in the equal importance of others, making the children feel that they are, as it were, answerable to somebody.

Different stages of a child's development often call for a different view of his actions. The action may be similar to one performed at another time or at another stage of his development, but the motive or the idea behind it may be different. Christian, at the age of eleven, became preoccupied with the meaning of order – with the purpose behind much of the skeletal structure that is embodied in family life. Typically he began to question the organisation of things. At the same time Paul, unable at four and a half to make any basic rational judgements about such things, found any disruption of the ritual of family life thoroughly disagreeable. For a while the brothers, so close, found each other's actions irritating. It was only by explaining to Christian the vital importance to Paul of ritual that their parents were able to restore harmony.

For ritual is a vital and continuing part of the developing process in the child up to the age of six. Life is governed by a series of rituals, from bed-time stories to teeth-cleaning, which, by forming a series of unquestioned areas, help in restricting the number of directions in which development is simultaneously directed. The strength of this ritual often overbears other, softer emotional patterns. For instance, Paul was accustomed to pretending to steer when going for rides in a friend's car. Ruth wanted a turn but he refused to give it to her – not, as a superficial observer might have supposed, because he was being selfish, but because to do so would have represented the disruption of a comforting and essential ritual. He knew that he was being unfair and that he was depriving Ruth of a turn, but the accustomed order of things was more important than hurting the sensibilities of his adored sister. By understanding this, and explaining it to Ruth, Maria was able to avoid an impossible confrontation with Paul. It wasn't that he didn't want to give his sister a turn, but that at his stage of development he was incapable of doing so.

Often the problem of self-discipline is increased by a difficulty in accepting direction through language – to children, terms and instructions which may seem simple to adults, can fail to have as concrete or developed a meaning as they have for adults. They may need to experience a course of action first and then to verbalise its advantages and disadvantages. Paul, being asked not to play a particular record – *Eine Kleine Nachtmusik* – over and over again, declined to accept the restriction till he had tried the course out himself. For two whole days the house echoed to the sound of the record. Paul was experiencing the effect of over-exposure to the music for himself, not simply accepting an adult interdiction at its face value. The rest of the family tolerated the resulting musical torture, and after a while Paul stopped, satisfied in his own mind that repeating the same piece of music too often *does* become an unpleasant experience, and free from any of the violence and frustrations that a blank refusal enforced with sanctions would have been found to generate in him. This is a particularly good example of the purpose of the prepared environment and the attitudes of mind created by Maria. Without isolation, understanding and the full participation of the other members of the family it could not have been carried through. As it was, once Maria and Martin had explained to Paul's siblings why he needed to play the record over and over again, they unquestioningly allowed him to continue, only expressing relief when the ordeal was over.

Discipline isn't a one-sided matter – something flowing only from the parent. It is a positive two-way social contact in which both sides must be prepared to participate. Children must be actively involved in deciding how their day should be apportioned: what amount of time should be given to pure play, what amount to school-play; the best times for rising and bedding and so forth. If the ritual is a self-imposed ritual, it is bound to become a stronger one than a rule of conduct imposed purely for parental convenience.

Young children are by nature egocentric; that is simply a fact of their make-up in the early stages of their development. Neither sanctions nor scolding will channel small children into patterns dictated by parental attitudes towards society. Their egocentricity must be accepted as natural and then be channelled later into socially desirable patterns. Above all they should be surrounded by purposeful patterns of behaviour which are in themselves educational. The controlled and prepared environment can prove a great help in this endeavour. Later on, when the child is better able to verbalise, it becomes possible to discuss egocentric behaviour in relation to whatever disruptive effect it may have on other members of the family. Until then it must be accepted without question and without producing special pressure on the child. Everything, however 'selfish' or maddening it may seem, has a positive as well as a negative side and should be made use of as part of the process of growing up. *Rituals*, part of the learning process in themselves, are constructive. *Rules*, being imposed for adult convenience, or at least based on adult criteria, are often unconstructive. Sometimes rituals seem to lead nowhere – all children indulge in such things as avoiding the lines between paving stones, balancing on things, or babbling. But even if they seem irritating or disruptive to other members of the family, they should be accepted and made part of a larger mother-child ritual, enriching the relationship in the form of shared play, or private jokes or secrets.

Sometimes in a crisis of co-operation it is important to let the rituals provide the necessary sheet anchor by allowing the essentially comforting nature of the familiar to take over and restore calm. For example, 'let's tidy up' is often an excellent way out of an impasse. Once Paul, refusing to give proper turns on the bicycle to his sister, was diverted by being allowed to become part of the family ritual of cooking. Maria gave him shelf-space and materials, and allowed him to participate. Almost at once he felt able to co-operate with Ruth over the bicycle. There had been no tears, no recriminations, only understanding by Maria, patience from Ruth, and a constructive solution. It was an ideal example of how constructively to gain co-operation. Egocentricity is almost always illogical – and thus demands a tangential approach to its solution.

Parents, too, are sometimes at fault, and there should be no difficulty or inhibition felt in showing the child that this is so. But at the same time care should be taken to impress the fact that faults committed by either adult or child are never the single responsibility of one party and if amends seem appropriate they should operate as fully on the child's side as on the adult's.

Both the child and the parent must be aware that at about five years the child becomes able to come to terms with logical analysis of his actions. Before that age Maria tries to cultivate rituals and games which make the child aware of the fact that we are all other than pure examples of self. Thus prepared, when the child becomes able to make logical rather than illogical judgements, he sometimes produces insights that will be quite dazzling. Once, after he had obtained an object he especially coveted from Ruth, Paul, after a few moments, said: 'It isn't worth having things just for oneself – they don't change colour because of that!' Later, after freely sharing a treasure with his brothers and sister, he said quite literally: 'If there isn't really "mine and yours", then me and you don't exist separately.'

Creativity is also a potent factor in the forging of children. The very act of creation – be it painting or composition or handicrafts – presupposes that the child is in itself unified. Creation demands full co-ordination, physically and mentally. Sometimes the refusal of a child to enter into 'family life' is caused more by some failing in that life itself than in the child. At other times it may prove necessary to accept the child, refusal and all, into the family, explaining to his siblings the necessity for this before they react aggressively or critically. Only then will the difficulty begin to iron itself out. That a child should have its own personal creative outlet is highly desirable, especially if it is one that does not put it in competition with other members of the family: sibling rivalry would be inevitable if, for instance, two of the children played the piano. It is no accident that Christian and Adam have become committed to different disciplines, and maintain more stoutly than truthfully that they understand nothing of the other's speciality. Christian claims to be tone deaf, and at school bellows loudly and tunelessly when confronted with the customary barrage of Welsh tunes. Adam, at the sight of a page of figures, rises silently and leaves the room. As a case of avoidance of sibling rivalry it is almost classic.

The conventional parent reading most of this will feel profoundly that it is 'unnatural', and that children not only enjoy rivalry, competition and occasional cathartic bursts of violence, but that they display unnatural traits if they don't at times behave at worst 'badly' and at best 'mischievously'. Indeed, for some people 'manliness' and anti-social conduct are synonymous. Probably such a parent would be unable to accept that Maria's children aren't 'naughty' with the same frequency and intensity as their own. The answer is – always excepting violence, from which they seem remarkably free – that they often are. It is simply that neither their mother nor their siblings accept this terminology (as Paul's failure to know the word 'naughty' strikingly showed).

Before the age of five, Maria concentrates on discovering the motivation of what are essentially egocentric forces in a child, and then attempts at best to canalise them, at worst to assimilate them. After this stage has been passed, reason is applied, and anti-social acts are analysed and then acted out. If, as sometimes happens (though with less frequency than most conventional parents would accept) truly wrong acts are committed by the children, then they are encouraged to make restitution of their own free will. The children invariably do this voluntarily and with a true sense of contrition. And in the act of restitution they seem quite genuinely to purge their act. Guilt is almost as foreign to them as is violence – especially since they have been taught, and believe, that ill-conduct is a two-sided responsibility and that the fault is almost invariably shared.

The children are not totally similar in this – Adam is the most certain that his concept of justice and restitution is right. Christian is the least certain – the most willing to compromise on questions of morality, to make intellectually justifiable but morally uncertain fringe judgements such as resorting to violent sarcasm rather than fisticuffs in the schoolroom context. Ruth and Paul, whose day-to-day morality is still bounded by home, fully accept a system based not on the idea of transgression but on one of reversible deviation from the process, and of sanctions which take the form of self-imposed restitution. If by the word 'discipline' is meant 'what punishments does Maria use?' that is the answer. If to you the word means 'what does she do when the children are naughty?' the answer is, tell them they have passed the borders of acceptable conduct, discuss the fault and what provoked it, and leave it to them to make good, as they inevitably do. It should be remembered that violent sanctions, or indeed any form of conventional discipline, is self-devaluing. Boys who are caned will still scrump apples – and find in the violent contact with their parents at least a contact of some sort. A family formed by children who constantly 'step over the line' and are repelled is an untranquil one, like a constant desert war in an arid sheikdom – and about as conducive to education. If Maria was asked what single precept was the most important, she would answer freedom from outside pressures, be they of guilt or violence or doubt, and a feeling of total 'togetherness' with the children. Only then are the mother and the children able to give themselves totally to the process of education.

For the rest, a summary would be as follows.

(a) *Environment* – in itself simply a cocoon allowing for this freedom from outside pressures which is of such paramount importance.

(b) *Freedom from objectives* – the release from any pressure to success or early achievement of educational goals. Quite literally, the course must be one of *laissez-faire* – the child should choose its own speed and the parent simply see that its footsteps don't falter on the way.

(c) *A reciprocal approach* – rather than an authoritative one. By recognising the early egocentricity of a child and helping it rather than opposing it, vital energy is spared, both by the child and the mother. This will then lead to a speedier embarkation on the seas of true education.

(d) *Self-sacrifice by the parents* – only by giving themselves totally to the 'process' can parents hope to succeed. The release from inner pressures of this surrender, the freedom from guilt about 'doing the best thing for the children' can make this sacrifice less difficult than the uninvolved would suppose.

Why does Maria believe 'the process' to be effective and make the almost superhuman effort necessary to practise it? Superficially the reason might seem the remarkable intellectual attainments of her children. But what for others would be grounds for wild self-congratulation, for her is only a by-product of a child who has become truly happy. Furthermore she believes passionately in non-competitiveness and is profoundly unimpressed by examination results and public acclaim. Now that her children have been freed from the pressures of violence and guilt it seems quite natural to Maria that they should get on well with their work, be it playing the piano or understanding mathematical concepts. It is easy, of course, to see in Maria's own childhood rejections and the negation of learning she suffered at the hands of a sadistic governess, the root of 'the process'. It is the antithesis of what she herself suffered.

But her overt motives are more complex than that – and as remarkable in themselves as the tremendous strength of will that has enabled her to carry on in the face of such enormous physical and financial difficulties. It is true that these difficulties have from time to time threatened to overwhelm her and that she has suffered periods of psychological disruption and acute mental and physical exhaustion. But a lesser woman would never have embarked on a scheme whose basic precepts involved total isolation and total self-sacrifice, and it is hard to imagine anybody else with the strength, albeit engendered by the unswerving calm and commitment of her husband, to carry such burdens for upwards of ten years.

Maria's main motive is simply this: she believes that she is educating a new type of person, that her children aren't simply precocious, or even, as is often suggested, geniuses. She sees them as 'free' – in the eighteenth century sense of *homme libre*. As the result of the 'process' they have no violence in them, no irrational guilt – quite simply are free of the feeling that stirs in all our bones in the darker watches of the night that we are somehow obscurely guilty of an original sin. What most of us see as a faintly embarrassing abstract concept of the total power of love, has been for Maria the basis of ten years cut off from the social life and patterns she wishes and hopes one day to indulge in again – music, painting and a dialogue with like-minded people.

She writes, and means it with every drop of sweat shed in ten years of standing as a rock-like shield between her children and the pressures of the world outside: *'Love is the intuition of the unity of all reality – we must foster this faith in ourselves – love in action is to act out this intuition to the end.'*

What Maria believes she has been doing is gaining an understanding of the delineating limits of human conduct, and then trying consciously to bring up her children so as to avoid any such limitations. She knew she must, as it were, take the day when it was most malleable – when a baby was only just born – and try to persuade it into a mould fashioned so as to avoid such flaws as violence, greed and rivalry. The tools she has used were chosen partly by intuition, partly from the teaching of mystic philosophers rather opaque in their expressed meaning, and partly from the good old-fashioned mother's method of trying and seeing. But it was never a random process, for everything possible was thought out. She started on this even before she met Martin, and they continued it together at Rome University before they married. Montessori, it is true, provided many of the tools; but nobody else considered possible her challenge to the whole conception of the darker aggressive sides of human behaviour. Science believes them to be regrettable but ever present elements under a veneer, thick or thin, of civilisation. Maria believed that if she built a prepared environment of sufficient strength, and then brought up the children in the way she knew to be right, many undesirable emotions could be *eliminated*, and that what we mostly accept as being 'natural' could be shown to be the product of avoidable strains during very early development.

Up to the present she has been successful – the children are as strikingly *different* as their upbringing has been; and different in quality as well as in educational excellence. Professional outsiders tend to take the view that this very difference is in itself dangerous for the children; that far from representing the vanguard of a new type of individual, as their mother hopes, they are bound to become social casualties. The argument is simple – they are so qualitatively apart, that when the time comes not only to leave their mother but also to come into contact with the outside world, they will be unable to cope.

The first part of this view misunderstands what Maria has tried to do. At no time has she tried to link the children inexorably with herself. Her only endeavour has been to bring them up strong enough to cope with alien social and moral pressures when they are older. There is as yet no reason to believe that she has bound them too close to herself, although by selecting an environment so deliberately cut off from externals she has clearly risked their becoming excessively attached to it and to her, whatever her conscious motives may have been.

The precocious mental development of the children does, however, make it difficult for them to find points of contact with their peers at school, and the type and nature of the games they play, and their innocence of television make assimilation into playground culture difficult. Some of Christian's choicest invective is kept for the games played by his classmates at his village primary school, particularly for 'Best Dier', where they all used to pretend to be shot. According to him it was 'a very *foolish* game' in the exact sense of the adjective.

Outsiders detect in the children a certain gaucheness, a dearth of 'please' and 'thank-you', a lack of 'manners' which reinforces the opinion of those who feel that the children are not 'of this world'. But conventional manners are unimportant, and are easily picked up later. All they really lack is a few key words of conventional social intercourse, and since they are impeccable in true concern for their fellows it seems probable that the superficial lack will prove a temporary disability.

What the future holds for Maria's children is inevitably a sterile debate – only time will resolve it. No sensible person can doubt that there are shoals ahead – as there are for any child whatever his background – be they academic hurdles, or the unavoidable strains of puberty. Some of these will be heightened by their unconventional upbringing and academic advancement, some diminished or subtly diverted into lesser and more complex channels. For instance, Christian is unlikely to be troubled by 'A' levels, but may well find it difficult to cope with the problems of an adolescence free from the self-deceptive cocoon in which many children seek and find protection. Adam, although rapt in music to the exclusion of almost everything, may find his first real rejection by a teacher or a colleague terribly wounding, while Ruth may find that the total trust she offers the strangers who come into her life may one day be cruelly confounded.

One or more of these things may happen – or perhaps like Galahad they will be saved from the worst of these problems by the strength of their inner purity. Their mother, undeterred by criticism of a course of education to which she was unable to envisage an alternative, believes that they will endure and multiply. There is no way of telling who is right. By its very nature this book can only be an interim report; one that might, with interest, be followed up in say five years time. As the man said when he fell from a ten storey building – 'so far – so good'.

Another question which is frequently asked is –'How intelligent are the children, really? Won't they simply blow up, overheat their brains, turn into vegetables?' Such questions profoundly fail to understand the true nature of intellectual activity, or the quality of achievement already obtained by the two elder children. They may lose interest in formal academic or musical discipline, or, for instance, become preoccupied with other things during adolescence. But it is likely to be a temporary diversion if it does occur at all, and would in no way detract from the solid intellectual achievement that they have already displayed. Christian's intellectual quality is one of clarity and conceptual thinking – something which is very unlikely to desert him. His development up till now demands, of course, further education leading at the earliest possible time to high formal qualifications. What *is* outside the scope of logical deduction is the ultimate quality of his achievement. Is he destined to hold a chair of mathematics with quiet distinction, or to uncover a fundamental truth that will serve to unlock the secrets of the universe? Is he to become a respected professor or a major innovator? The answer must lie in his further development. At present all one can say is that he is on the launching pad, and that almost anything seems to be possible for him.

The same is true of Adam. But musicians are born and not the product of a style of education, and nobody who has spent time with Adam, or heard him play, doubts for one instant that within him are considerable wells of purest talent. But the progress of the musician is more fraught with pitfalls than that of an academic. In the world of professional music there is little place for the merely competent pianist, while the competition to become an international virtuoso is waged with an intensity that makes the rivalry to become Capo of the Mafia seem restrained by comparison. To succeed one needs not only talent and financial backing, but also luck – being in the proverbial right place at the right time, and so on. Adam's teachers believe that he has the inner quality of musicianship that is the God-given gift and without which nothing is possible. He is industrious almost to a fault, and has an abundance of the quality which his mother seems almost above all to have imparted to her children – that of high seriousness. For him the piano is not simply a means of expression, it is an extension of his inner being. 'Mummy,' he said when he was only six, 'when I die I want you to put my piano under the ground with me.' Sometimes he expresses sentiments of vocation which in a child of his age seem faintly comical—until one realises that for him they are deadly serious. Adam has all the gifts and a nascent technique the development of which now reposes in capable hands. But unlike Christian, he will need pure luck to conquer his chosen Everest. There are, however, already outsiders who believe that they can detect in him signs of the quality which separates a potential Rubinstein from a future professor of piano in a provincial conservatoire, and perhaps luck will be steered his way.

Ruth and Paul are too young as yet to have launched into careers or chosen specific paths, which makes speculation about them unfruitful. But they too will choose, with their mother's attention and help, to follow courses which will lead them into contact with the pressures attendant on achieving success outside the family circle. Then, brought up in an atmosphere free from competition, they will have to learn to live with such instincts on the part of others, and perhaps to suffer rejections and attempted manipulation foreign to the very nature of the life in which they have been brought up. All will depend on the strength of their preparation, on the flowering of the seeds that Maria has so dedicatedly sown.

Much of the outside interest in the upbringing of the children concerns their scholastic achievements. Parents harried by a system of education which places so much value on passing exams must look with wonder at an eleven year old child who can pass, as Christian did, his qualifications for university entrance in the space of a couple of months. Did Maria cause Christian's precocious development, would any child brought up by her process make such startling progress? A straight answer isn't easy. Clearly the situation must be compounded of a combination of genetic inheritance and environment-influenced development. The question how these two things relate is one of the oldest and bitterest battlegrounds of science.

Maria's own view is the simple and probably correct one that her children are genetically endowed with considerable intelligence, and that 'the process', with its freedom from such diversions as television and comics, and from what she sees as the debilitating tension arising from aggression and violence, has allowed them an untrammelled development. Whether this has simply resulted in an early flowering, or whether the tree is on the way to growing stronger and taller than it would otherwise have been, is debatable.

Christian, for instance, has time to assimilate enough formal mathematical information to allow, even if his rate of progress normalises, for his attaining most ordinary academic goals at a remarkably early age. He and the others *have* been made into educational super-children. But although this has happened, one must bear in mind that it wasn't the aim of 'the process'. The freedom from pressures, the constant attention, were designed to produce children of a certain *moral character* and not simply of educational excellence, which for Maria is only a by-product, unimportant in an ethos free from competitiveness. The parent who considers bringing up his child by 'the process' can expect his offspring's intellectual development to be enhanced – but they would also be different children, with a different psychological make-up. It is this which is of paramount importance to Maria, while educational achievement is only an extension of the capabilities of the truly happy child. Many parents would see the order of priorities the other way round.

We may well ask if there is a lesson in this family's story so far which might be applicable to the upbringing of our own children. Maria's answer is simple: 'There is Truth here. Attempt the Kingdom and all else will be given to you. Attempt it, and the wells of strength will flow and all will be possible.'

Perhaps the more rational answer is that there is food for thought – not only for those who have the keeping of small children in primary schools, but also for every parent struggling to bring up children in an environment over which he may have less than perfect control. What every mother knows instinctively in her very bones – that love is all and that any separation from her child is separation from herself – is true. With strength such as Maria's one can break the chains and change the accepted patterns of upbringing, and the results are, to say the least, remarkable.

74

When a child cries in the night, or maddens with repeated 'naughtiness', let its parents reflect, and let Maria's Process help them, even if only imperfectly, to give it some of the gifts bestowed on Christian, Adam, Ruth and Paul.

CHAPTER FIVE

CHRISTIAN

Christian is about four feet six inches tall and eleven years old. His face is dominated by his enormous pale grey eyes, their slightly pink lids shielded by pale eyelashes so long that they brush his cheeks. His head is covered with tangles of mouse-coloured hair, tufted like an ill-knotted doormat. Furthermore Christian's teeth stick out like a beaver's. He moves awkwardly, his elbows sticking out, and constantly utters, rather abstractedly, cries of: 'oh, ooh, oooh'. His air is that of a highly intelligent insect.

It's surprising to discover that underneath this eccentric, professorlike exterior Christian is a strongly built, solid little boy who, if he had the mind for it, could make a footballer or a fine tree-climber. But taking it by and large he has not the mind for it. His interests are almost all cerebral. And when Christian is reading or working his concentration is total – all the children share this trait. Oblivious to the cries of his younger brother, or the piano playing of Adam, Christian diverts himself during his free time with a balanced and satisfying equation, a copy of *The Scientist* or an article reassessing Einstein's theory of relativity. When he is reading you can talk to him, or pummell him, or stand on your head in front of him without the slightest diversionary effect. When he finishes an article or a mathematical problem, it is almost as though he is returning from a deep sleep. He blinks, exclaims, and seems to have to reorientate himself to the objects in the room.

But if he is dedicated in the exact sense of the word to his mathematics, neither his temperament nor his aura is cold or withdrawn. Christian is also likely to pass an afternoon playing wholeheartedly with his brothers and sister, or freely to push aside a treatment of the quantum theory in order to paint, to write a poem, or to build a model aircraft, often with Paul.

His most frivolous diversion is science fiction. Not merely a simple connoisseur, he is a critic. He is still full of contempt for the author who told him that heavy water was an isotope of hydrogen, or that a galaxy existed in a spot already amply occupied by a recently detected body. He drives his way through anything and everything the local library can provide with a speed which results in a constant problem. His reading speed is an astonishing two hundred pages an hour – a capacity that allows him easily to devour two books a day – and a Council regulation allows a child only two library tickets. At weekends, desperate for something to read, Christian will sometimes visit the library twice in a single day, making an eclectic but highly serious selection of reading matter.

Christian's intelligence burns with a cold blue flame. His judgement of other people is severe, and one might think his standards too high, his regard too unblinkingly frank, were not these the same standards that he applies to himself.

But it can prove unnerving to adults, especially those cushioned with a veneer of self esteem. A casual remark to Christian can elicit such replies as: 'That's a very silly question! Do you mean A or B or C or a combination of the first two?' His presence, which is totally adult, engenders precise thinking in those around him. He is disconcertingly direct, asks what he wants to know, expects a direct reply and rejects those unable to supply the information he requires. To those who don't know Christian, it is often very frightening.

For instance, when he was in Cambridge on his way to visit the university computer, a film cameraman joined the boy as he was having his supper in a restaurant. It was probably the first meal Christian had eaten in so luxurious a public place, but he didn't appear to notice the plush and gilt surroundings at all. He gazed abstractedly out of the window, and from time to time helped himself clumsily from the enormous plate of vegetables handed by the tail-coated waiter.

'Enjoying yourself, are you son?' the cameraman asked.

It was the first time they'd met – nobody addresses Christian like that after they have been with him ten minutes. Christian appeared not to notice. Then he suddenly focused on the cameraman.

'Can I ask you a question?' he demanded – Christian seldom, if ever, says 'please'.

'Of course.'

'Do the ion particles in the light accelerate when they strike your lens, and does this affect the colour layers in the film itself?'

Silently the cameraman rose from the table, gazed in wonderment at the child and stalked back to the rest of his crew to pass the evening in easier company.

Next day, Christian was scheduled to visit the radio telescope at Cambridge, a place pregnant with the atmosphere of the many important scientfic discoveries which have been made there. As usual he was uninterested in his surroundings, seemingly oblivious to the beauty of the black radio-bowls etched against the blue sky.

'I want to go inside,' he demanded. Unfortunately the doors were locked, awaiting the arrival of a distinguished scientist who had agreed to explain his laboratories to the visitors. Finally he arrived on the omnipresent Cambridge bicycle, his face pink and friendly, his left leg still protectively sheathed by a bicycle clip. He beamed at the mob of people waiting at the door and began, in a great hurry, to explain about the telescope. His manner was kind, but clearly he believed that it was a waste of his valuable time to come eight miles on a bicycle on a windy day, simply in order to explain to a rather odd-looking small boy the highly technical workings of his department.

Christian became more and more gawky. He stood on one leg, he scratched his ear. His pale eyes focused on the middle distance.

'You know that the difference between a star and a planet is that one twinkles when you look at it through a telescope. . .' explained the astronomer in a flat voice.

Christian looked out of the window.

'Can I ask you a question?' he then asked.

'Of course.' The astronomer was grateful at having elicited even a faint show of interest.

'Why does the pulsar in the Crab nebula cease when there is an eclipse of the moon?'

There was a long silence. The astronomer took a pencil from his pocket and began to explain on a piece of paper. Soon it was covered in mathematical equations. Christian selected a pen from the collection in the breast pocket of his school blazer and began to write too. The rest of the company was lost as the two of them discussed imploded galaxies. But Christian too was lost in his element, suddenly totally absorbed in what he was doing, no longer gawky or disinterested. In an adult conversation about a subject of fascination to him, Christian was truly 'at home'.

Some adults feel Christian is 'above himself' and needs 'taking down a peg'. Essentially they have misunderstood the child. Christian takes as cold a view of himself as he does of the outside world. He knows that he is clever but he also knows his own limitations and failures and can live with them without the padding of self-deception that many of us need. He expects the same of others – but remains a generous, concerned companion, even if he is one who needs more getting to know that most children of eleven. Christian has the Roman virtues – courage, high moral standards, and considerable self-knowledge. Others, alas, sometimes find them uncomfortable to behold.

When Christian was born, his coming was a great cementing for his parents. Until then everything seemed to have been against them. Every possible form of opposition had been thrown in their path by Maria's family, and this baby boy was an answer to their prayers. Literally, he was Christian, the sign that 'God is with us' in our journey. But things still were far from easy, and as he grew older they seldom seemed to be improving.

He was nearly two when his parents went to live in a community. He would lie on his back in an upper room, while his mother tried to cook and clean for a giant household, and the child was quickly bored. In desperation, his mother hung amusing objects from hooks in the ceiling above where he lay, so that he would have something to occupy himself while she worked. Able to distinguish between colours before he could talk, Christian would colour-code a set of plastic milk bottles for hours, making neat piles and then rearranging them.

As he grew older, Maria found that the only way to keep the child occupied was by carrying him everywhere while she cooked. He sat like a parcel on her hip, his enormous eyes absorbing everything and everybody. Within months he was constantly demanding to be read to, and cooking and reading became a combined activity in the community kitchen. Christian toddled around as soon as he was able, making friends with the disparate members of the Community – asking them all questions and receiving from each his own separate kind of answer. It was perhaps unsettling – some members were better able to communicate with the curious child than others were, some evinced more patience and understanding than others. Difficult in many ways, it was also a rich environment, full of adults each able to satisfy some section of his curiosity. In spite of the somewhat unsettling atmosphere, Christian seemed to be an essentially ordinary intelligent toddler, taking an interest in everything and anything around him.

Then when Christian was four and a half, Maria took the children back to her native Italy. For the children it was partly a holiday and partly a strange kaleidoscopic experience of a foreign land, populated by strange relations, speaking a strange language. Adjustment was not always easy. It was here however that Christian's father first noticed that his eldest son had an unusual mathematical turn of mind. The family were shopping, buying potatoes in the market. It was full of all the colour and excitement of an Italian street. Martin bought a kilogram and a half, handed over a note and got some change. The four-year-old Christian remarked that it worked out at fifty lire a kilo. It was a complex calculation and Martin was rightly astonished that a four year old could master it.

At this period, Martin was studying in the evenings for his 'A' levels in mathematics, trying to fill profitably the time while he was in Italy, and planning to take the exam when he got back to England. Christian was fascinated by the textbooks, by the paraphernalia of geometry and calculation, and by the shapes of graphs, the actual physical look of mathematical symbols and equations. He invented games, in one of which he would run to the edge of a space and shout 'limit'. It was only a child's game but already Christian had grasped a mathematical concept, and was aware that there was more to sums than simply adding rows of numbers or doing simple calculations.

Martin continued working for his 'A' levels when they returned to England, and Christian continued to be fascinated by the secret and exciting games his father seemed to be playing. Sometimes he would come and play in the room where Martin was working and ask questions. Gently and patiently Martin would always find the time to stop and to answer. Soon the child could understand such problems as long division, grasping quickly concepts which children years older often have difficulty in mastering. But the process of learning was simple. The child would ask; his father – curious to see how much his son could absorb – would reply to his questions, and gently explain the concept.

If Christian showed no interest, no attempt was made to interest him. Above all there was absolutely no pressure, no desire to teach the boy to perform tricks. His father watched and waited and much of the time Christian played the play of children of his age.

One day, just before he was seven, Christian discovered his father's logarithm tables. He demanded to know what they were for. Martin explained – here was a way that one could change the onerous tasks of multiplication and division into the comparatively easy ones of addition and subtraction. It was like a magic game, and Christian understood it at once. He looked at the different columns and began to use the tables, settling down to it with little or no fuss. Martin was astonished by the speed with which his young son grasped the uses and facilities of the log tables. Together they skipped to the five figure tables. So speedy, so unsensational and 'natural' was Christian's progress that Martin could see no purpose in wasting time with four figure ones.

From there it was only a short natural step to square roots. Martin showed the child the old, longhand method. Christian instantly realised that in the logs there was an easy shortcut. He began to manifest a characteristic impatience with mathematical long-windedness. If the route from A to B was tortuous there must be a simpler way of finding it, less demanding of his valuable time. He began to experiment. At seven, he understood cube roots, progressed to the square of cube roots and then soon after, to fractional roots. Mathematics became for Christian a deeply fascinating game.

But there were dormant periods too, and still nobody pushed him. Martin, anyway, was primarily absorbed in passing his exams, and Maria had two other small children to cope with. For days at a time Christian ignored mathematics. Then Martin would think of a paradox – something curious which he felt would appeal to Christian – and father and son would play with a mathematical problem, as some children play with a toy.

Bit by bit Christian began to grasp the rudiments of algebra and one day his father showed him how to draw out equations on squared paper, showing their natural balance in graphic representation. Christian was interested and began to divert himself with monstrous sums. How many atoms are there in the world? How many thousand tons do whales weigh? How many grains of sand are there in the Sahara? What is the average specific density of the world? It was the cerebral equivalent of collecting train numbers, of plane spotting, or hoarding bus tickets. So isolated was the house on the hill, so unrelated to the educational structure of the outside world, that Martin was not aware how unusual these games were. He simply did not know how few children at six or seven can work with five figure logs, or understand quadratic equations.

On his ninth birthday, Christian set about verifying some of the laws governing the universe. He would not accept such concepts as gravity, or the speeds of light or sound, until he had examined them and proved them. He began with Kepler's Law – that the orbit of a planet is proportional to the square of the inverted cube of the distance. Thwarted in his attempt to disprove this, and content to admit after direct observation that the great eighteenth-century astronomer had not been at fault, he turned his attention to other Laws, then to an endless string of quadratic equations.

His father presented him with the theory: with a quadratic equation you have got two perfectly valid answers and you can arrive at them in a variety of ways. Christian was fascinated. His father showed him more. They passed on to 'complex numbers' and it was a revelation for the child. His father left him to contemplate the possible permutations, and Christian returned to him again and again with paradoxes he had found and alternate answers which he had arrived at, with the same delight as most children would display over a coloured stone or a piece of glass, or a rare stamp.

Outside his mathematics obsession, the boy found time for other pastimes. He was also devouring books – science fiction, Tolkien, and popular scientific text books. Before he was ten his rate of reading was already about one hundred and fifty pages an hour. But still his parents never pushed him, allowing him complete freedom in the choice of what he would read, just as they allowed him full freedom in his playing. If Christian wanted to read or paint or simply do nothing, nobody thought of it as a more peculiar activity than playing with complex numbers. If he asked a question, Martin would find time to answer fully and patiently. If he didn't ask, nothing special was done to stimulate his curiosity.

When he was nine and a half, father and son began trigonometry. Christian devoured this too. At about this time, Martin was giving private lessons to some sixteen-year-old boys from the town. He became aware that his nine-year-old son could easily pass the 'O' level exam that they were floundering to prepare for. Furthermore, not content with standard and laborious procedures, Christian was for ever devising short cuts, finding quicker, more elegant ways of dealing with standard mathematical problems. Simple problems no longer really interested him. He was less and less prepared to play numbers, more and more curious about mathematical ideas, fascinated by such things as the theory of probability. Christian had begun on a road that was to lead him higher and higher into the realms of pure abstraction.

Of course, all this time, there was school. Christian bitterly resisted having to go. He hated it. From the age of six he had done everything he could to avoid going, short of actual physical refusal. He tried to reason: 'Mother, I go to school to learn things, don't I? But I already know everything they can teach me, so there is no point in my going.' 'If I was to fall into this ditch and break my leg, maybe then I wouldn't have to go to school.' Conscious of how little Christian was gaining at school, but also aware of the social consequences of keeping him at home, Maria, with terrible reluctance, took the child to school.

It was a tiny Welsh village school, two or three miles away over the turf-capped slag heaps, and she took him on foot. There in the morning and back home again every evening. Seven miles in all. The school was simple. In one big room most of the older pupils sat together. The senior age groups and streams were obliged to work higgledy-piggledy in one room. The master sat at a high desk at the end, dominating the children from his perch, as he had dominated their parents in their generation. What he taught did not interest Christian, and the way he taught was so different from Maria's methods that it seemed to the child meaningless and frightening.

Christian has forgiven this school nothing and has forgotten nothing. Even now he refuses to go inside the buildings, to come near its playing fields. When asked to talk about his first school he stood on the dark spoil heaps, peering down on the buildings in their blank asphalt playground through his astronomer's telescope. His figure on the skyline was like a piece of Giacometti sculpture, bent against the wind, his duffle coat blown around him.

They were evil memories. When he first went there he was just six. He understood five figure logs, he read one hundred and fifty pages an hour. On his first day the schoolteacher asked him if he could read. He answered directly and clearly but was taken to be boasting and was set to work on *Janet and John*, an elementary reading manual which seemed to him beneath contempt. In mathematics the child fared no better. Uninterested in simple sums and not particularly good at adding and subtracting, Christian's extraordinary precocity passed completely unnoticed.

Occasionally he scored small points, gaining from them perhaps a disproportionate amount of pleasure. He still recalls how once, in class, he raised his hand: 'Why are we wasting time with these silly sums when we are going decimal in 2.743 recurring years?' he asked.

With a bellow of rage Christian was despatched to pass the rest of the maths lesson in the corridor.

Christian's classmates were village children, neither better nor worse than the children from any small village. In the playground they played rowdy games, their favourite being Best Dier. A party of children mimed a machine-gun squad at dawn, and the most realistic death agonies in the playground dust gained the prize. Christian hated it. For him 'non-violence' wasn't an abstract creed espoused by his parents. It was simply a way of life. At home he never fought his brothers, never played with toy guns and at his most violent painted a picture entitled 'Bang – you are *not* dead'.

In the playground Christian stood slightly aloof and apart. Never using his fists, he nevertheless protected himself adequately with his tongue and his uncanny ability to sink into the background, able to escape with political cunning from threatening situations. By the standards of any village school he was unmanly, odd and unpredictable, and no doubt his teacher found him an unattractive little boy. In return Christian hated him.

Over his telescope Christian said, as he peered down on the school he had left six months before: 'Mr Jones was a paraschizoid with certain sadomasochistic tendencies.' When asked to elaborate he replied: 'You know what I mean. He was, clinically, a paraschizoid with certain sadomasochistic tendencies.'

'And what effect did that have?'

'Oh, all the boys used to have nightmares, wet their beds and come out in terrible rashes.'

'And how about you, Christian?'

The child grinned.

'Oh, you will have noticed I s-t-u-t-t-e-r all the time.'

Of course the teacher was no such thing, was no doubt trying to make the best of difficult circumstances. But Christian's unblinking eyes had taken in much and forgiven nothing.

When Christian and his classmates were old enough to take the eleven-plus examination to decide if they were to go on to grammar school, they were all put in for it but only some of them received special coaching as being likely prospects. Christian was not among those so favoured. He may well have been assessed as not needing it, but was convinced that boys were selected not on merit but because their parents were important people in the village – the dairy owner, the local shopkeeper, the postmaster and so on – and that he was being treated as a second class citizen. Whatever the truth of the matter, Christian passed and went, barely eleven years old, to the local grammar school in the town. In many ways he was lucky. The area of Wales where his family lives has been in control of a socialist council for many years, the legacy of the great slump, a tyrannical local ironmaster, and the fierce independence of the Welsh working classes. The grammar school, admittedly run by a council without a single Tory member, takes a high percentage of the pupils from the local primary schools – as high as forty or fifty per cent of the local children get a grammar school education. Christian went to the Castle Grammar School – an impressive early Victorian building, shaped like a Gothic castle in a high German fairy story. Formerly the home of the local ironmaster, it stands on a hill, dominating the town. Its owner once ran it like a medieval princeling a city state. Now its sharp Victorian outline, with turrets and battlements, stands grimly as a reminder that once the whole town – and everybody in it – belonged to one man. It is said that the local ironmaster's tomb bears the words: 'God forgive me'. It is also said by townspeople that he had done much which placed him in need of forgiveness.

From the first, Christian was not quite like the other pupils – he was gaucher, perhaps a little less used to the company of other boys, certainly less prepared for the rowdy give and take of a large grammar school. The other boys were tough and self-assured – used to a life on the unforgiving spoil heaps and at home to heavy talk of 'the bad old days'. These boys were wrapped up in a way of life already sharply delineated by the social structure of the area, and at first nobody really noticed Christian. He sank into the background, took on the protective colouring he had acquired at his village school so as to keep on the right side of his classmates.

At first he didn't seem to be exceptional in lessons. He was considered bright and promising, maybe, but nevertheless he failed to catch the teacher's eye in the same way as he had passed unnoticed through his previous school. But this time, Christian was very happy. The atmosphere at the grammar school was conducive to learning. The Welsh are proud – as many minorities are – of educational excellence, second only to the rugby field. The final class lists at university are the battleground of a proud race. And Christian, for the first time, was in an atmosphere in which it was considered proper to learn, where nobody – not even the heartiest athlete – mocked you because you read a textbook, and nobody considered it socially necessary to twist your arm because you wanted to learn something. In his own quiet way, Christian began to find his feet, and to gain confidence.

Although he didn't shine at the team games which his classmates so delighted in, he became part of the class – fulfilling in the structure of personalities the role of a tame but absent-minded professor. True, the other boys teased him, but they were fond of him. Christian began to relax – something he had never been able to do at his primary school. And now he repaid the teasing of his classmates with genuine affection. And Christian took a full part in the more intellectual part of school life. He wrote the class newspaper, started an astronomy club, joined the chess club where he played often with boys very much older than himself, for at chess Christian displays great – though not abnormal – talent.

But more important, it was also here that his true intellectual prowess was first noticed. The mathematics teacher, who also ran the chess club, came into the classroom to find

Christian passing a spare moment between matches demonstrating to a wide-eyed collection of sixth-formers the general proof of a quadratic equation. So short was Christian that he had to stand on a chair the better to write on the blackboard.

At first the teacher simply didn't believe his eyes. Christian was a first former of eleven and as such should more properly be working on long division. Yet here was the child calmly coping with a mathematical subject that he shouldn't really undertake until he was sixteen or seventeen. What is more, he appeared fully to understand the problem he was exposing to his wondering fellows, with the easy assurance of somebody who himself had long mastered this particular hurdle. His master watched him silently from the back of the class. Was this a party trick – something Christian had learned from a book – and was he now performing solely to impress the other boys? Dying with curiosity he waited till the boy had finished and then took Christian into a corner of the classroom and questioned him.

The more the teacher discovered, the more astonished he became. Christian seemed to know enough pure mathematics to pass at least his 'O' levels, though there were wide gaps. For instance he knew scarcely any trigonometry. But for a boy of his age, his mathematical knowledge was clearly phenomenal. What was more, he seemed to understand the concepts he had met with in his largely solitary progression through a series of mathematical text books, with a thoroughness which in itself was almost more exceptional than the breadth of his knowledge. Obviously some kind of special educational facilities were going to have to be provided for him – the ordinary maths classes of his eleven-year-old contemporaries would be worse than useless.

After anxious deliberation the school decided simply to act empirically, and to put Christian into the class commensurate with his mathematical ability whatever that might be at any given moment. So Christian found himself taking his mathematics in the sixth form – with boys six or seven years older than himself.

True, there were yawning gaps in his knowledge, gaps that the other boys in the senior class had long since filled. But now Christian began to devour mathematics at a rate which astonished everybody. Working after hours with his highly sympathetic teacher, for whom he soon developed a very genuine affection, the boy simply galloped through the textbook. Sometimes he would master in hours problems which other children took months to overcome. What was more, he appeared to understand perfectly what he was doing. Often, it is true, he didn't bother to work out the examples – simply reading the chapter and comprehending the problem and the scope of the difficulties before moving on to the next thing. This seemed to go against all good educational practice, but since Christian fully understood and was impatient to acquire new knowledge, he was allowed to find his own pace of progress.

Christian was difficult to satisfy. But once he was satisfied, once he had mastered a mathematical tool, he applied it with the sureness of somebody who had been using it for months rather than for hours. When he came to his teacher it was either because the question in the textbook was wrongly phrased or because the answer he had arrived at was not the same as the answer in the book – and in such instances it was invariably Christian who was right. From curiosity at his pupil's prowess his teacher turned to amazement – Christian was truly phenomenal.

One day, for instance, Christian came to him and said: 'I cannot understand the problem.'

It was a simple question most children in the sixth form understood easily. The teacher was amazed – Christian could surely manage this problem. The teacher explained.

'It is simple,' he said. 'A ball was dropped down a lift shaft, the lift rose, at what velocity did they meet? Surely *you* understand, Christian? It is a simple question of air acceleration of sixteen feet per second as the ball drops.'

'No,' said Christian, 'I don't see. There are two questions I must ask you. Firstly, how high are we above sea level?'

The teacher nodded—this was the sort of question any really bright pupil might ask – and replied: 'For the purpose of this problem we are at zero.'

Christian went on: 'Am I to assume that the falling ball inherits the inertia of the rising lift?'

This time the teacher was really amazed. This concept of inherited inertia was quite outside the scope of everyday sixth form mathematics. Christian had understood more by the question itself than the examiners could possibly have supposed. For an hour he tried to explain to Christian the difficult concept of inherited inertia – incidentally stretching his own professional competence to the utmost.

The boy grasped the concept – and, his curiosity slaked, the subject was closed. Not surprisingly, other children observed Christian with increasing awe. 'Our Professor' as they called him in his class, was clearly not just a credit to them and their school, he was an almost magical pheno- menon, taking it by and large far more entertaining than having a potential rugby star in the class. In mathematics they couldn't even comprehend the problems which Christian battled with. But instead of becoming jealous, they themselves tried harder. Other children in the class began to ask the teacher for advice on mathematical prob- lems they normally wouldn't have encountered for two or three years after having heard Christian talk about them. The teacher was delighted – having a 'genius' in the class was an almost unalloyed pleasure.

Christian, for the first time in his life, was really happy at school. In all ordinary subjects he was second or third in the class, while for mathematics he sat with the older boys in the sixth form, quietly preparing himself for the

Advanced level, which was designed to show that a pupil was ready at about seventeen to attend a university course. Christian was still not twelve. It was all very well for the moment, but obviously Christian's development would soon present terrible problems to his school. What was one to do with a child who, in eight or nine weeks, appeared to be able to master mathematical problems which children six or seven years older than himself could not master? Furthermore, if the tremendous rate of progress was continued, quite soon it was going to be hard, in the context of a normal school's curriculum, to cope with the kind of mathematics Christian would require. On the other hand, in other subjects his different and normal quality of work was bound to lead to a lopsided development which would preclude such easy solutions as an early transfer to university.

It is just this lop-sidedness that made it so difficult to envisage the best course for Christian. Typically the boy himself is totally aware of the problem. To the question: 'Wouldn't it be easier if you gave up maths, or at least spent less time on it, and gave more effort to other subjects? Surely then you would become more balanced and it would be easier for you to decide what to do.' Christian replied: 'I think it's possible that if I spent less time on maths and more time on other subjects I could get myself ahead of the other boys.' (Christian is never anything except totally frank.) 'But,' he added, 'I think they would give me rather a bad time, wouldn't they? It wouldn't be frightfully safe.'

Christian is shrewd enough to realise that in his case, social safety lies not in overall excellence but in disappearing over the academic horizon, so that the other boys would neither be envious nor try to get their own back on him in other ways.

While waiting to see what the next few months or even weeks brings, Christian's headmaster wisely believes that his development as a person is equally as important as his development as a scholar. This precludes an early entrance to university – he certainly should not go to university before he is sixteen or seventeen. On the other hand, if Christian is going to be taught mathematics – then especially qualified people will be needed for the task.

The problem was eased when we offered Christian a treat. When asked: 'What would you like to do most in the world?' Christian replied unhesitatingly, 'I would like to see a computer and be allowed to work on it.'

So it was arranged. And in Cambridge, which was chosen as an appropriate place for this encounter, it would be possible for him to meet adult mathematicians fully able to advise and help him.

Christian had seldom left home before. For him it was not only the realisation of an ambition but it was also a great adventure. Provided with a large pile of books – enough, at his going rate of two hundred pages an hour, to fill the long journey from Wales to Cambridge – Christian set off to meet the computer.

Oblivious as always of his surroundings, Christian looked neither to right nor to left out of the train windows. Towns slipped by without his even noticing they were there. For him the train journey was measured only by the pages of the science fiction he read.

Once in Cambridge, and at the Department of Applied Mathematics, Christian became agitated – something very rare. He paced up and down outside the computer room while things were being readied, demanding: 'What language does it speak? Until I know what language it speaks I shan't know what to say to it.'

'English,' someone answered.

Christian became crosser.

'*No* computer speaks English.' This was scorn.

'Am I to suppose that it is an analogue computer or am I to suppose that I should address it in edsac?'

We all looked blank. Finally Christian was let in. In a sense it was an anti-climax. He glanced at the flashing lights which played over the control panels. But now he showed no emotion. The Professor gently explained to him its workings. Christian comprehended. He asked two or three direct questions and then sat down at the keyboard. Within ten minutes he was totally absorbed programming the computer as though he had been there all his life, reacting, the staff said, like any mature student. Patiently he began to work out a question of resonance, irate only when the computer's workload delayed his programme.

As the afternoon wore on Christian's iron concentration began to manifest itself. He became oblivious of his surroundings, of the various people milling around him. When the time came for the laboratories to close, six or seven hours later, he was still absorbed, angry only that he should be unable to continue, anxious only to return the next day. Characteristically Christian's treat had been silent, private, and in many ways it had been less sensational than we, the bystanders, had hoped. He had mastered the basics of the computer with the same speed as he had mastered mathematical problems in the abstruse text books he read at home in the evenings to amuse himself.

Once back home in Wales, Christian started to devote himself to astronomy. He had been given a telescope. Now he passed hours peering through it and working out elaborate computations concerning the speed of light, and the distances separating galaxies. For the first time other boys became interested in Christian's projects. Egged on, perhaps, by their parents, they came to regard the play of their strange schoolmate as more significant than they had before. Christian began to instruct them. The relationship between them was correct, warm and comradely, but always Christian remained the teacher, they the pupils. They would come and play at his home, sometimes for hours, but it was Christian who explained to them what was going on, showed them the magic figures which they could hardly comprehend and pointed out the excitements and the fascination of the distant stars they could see from the telescope. And when his friends returned to the cottages from which they came, their parents would pride themselves that something had rubbed off on them and one day they would grow up to be like Christian.

None of this changed the atmosphere around Christian inside his home, and he himself hardly seemed to notice what was going on. Sometimes he would drop his book of calculus and spend hours playing with his younger brother. It was for Paul that Christian, unable to think of any other way of keeping his younger brother quiet while he worked, wrote his book of poems and illustrated them.

Sometimes Christian and Paul would play games for hours together, sometimes they would paint pictures, sometimes they would all go for long walks – Christian putting on one side the abstract problems that had exercised his mind in the morning and playing simple games of make-believe with his younger brothers and sister. He is capable of childish flights of imagination and fantasy, as well as of the mature thought necessary for a university student.

In spite of all his achievements, Christian remains endearingly bad at arithmetic. One day as I talked to him, he multiplied three sevens wrong, making it twenty-eight. I pointed it out. At once he invented a complicated reason why he was right, based on an eight-figure system. It was a striking demonstration of the exact nature of his mathematical talents. The present state of knowledge supposes that there are two specific kinds of mathematically gifted children; those capable of abstract mathematical thought, and figuring children – that is children who can make enormous calculations in their heads, tell you how many days it is to their next birthday, how many weeks it is before the end of the century and then double it and multiply by five million.

Christian is incapable of such feats. His is the talent which allows him to understand the pure abstract mathematical concepts which other children of eleven would find as incomprehensible as Sanskrit. And as a general rule this is the kind of talent that does not seem to burn out. This kind of child will continue on the same mathematical level until either his imagination leads him into other paths, or he becomes a professional mathematician. Christian's talent is not unique – but it is truly exceptional in that it is developed at his age to an extraordinarily advanced degree.

Unlike the rest of his family, Christian is acutely aware of the outside world, sensitive through his schoolmates to such things as television, advertising and newspapers. He takes a keen, if cool interest in international affairs, sometimes plunging into despair over such things as Biafra or indulging in semi-scientific states of gloom over pollution or the exploding birthrate. Sometimes for days at a time Christian will be gloomy because, he says, there won't be enough food to go round by the time he is an adult, or because man is using pesticides too freely. Additionally Christian is also aware of money and is interested in business. But when he himself comes by a sum of money he almost invariably gives it away – buying presents for brothers and sister. Christian's attitude to money is like his attitude to many other things: cool, logical and completely unforgiving either of himself or others.

Christian's major handicap is his age. He is simply too young to make use of his gifts in the accepted social context. An old head on young shoulders is often unattractive – and those who haven't seen him with his siblings often take him to be a slightly malevolent gnome. In time he will become better able to make use of his gifts – and to scale who knows what heights. In the meantime he must be protected from too much pain and allowed to draw support from his remarkable family.

CHAPTER SIX

ADAM

When I first came to talk to Adam, his elder brother Christian said: 'The last person to talk to Adam got 1.173 recurring words in reply to each question.'

'Good,' said I. 'At least that's better than receiving only one word in reply to each question.'

'Well,' said Christian, 'for three questions Adam said nothing, but for another he said yes I think so – that puts up the average.'

Adam is nine, an almost incredibly slender child. He gives an impression of such frailty that one is in serious doubt for his health. He has enormous blue-grey eyes, which dominate his face, and a cropped fringe like a prep-school child in the nineteen-thirties – an impression reinforced by slightly old-fashioned, loosely fitting clothes, and Oxford bags for trousers.

Adam is the kind of child every mother wants to fold in her arms – appealing, frail and apparently in need of instant mothering. Mostly he hardly talks at all, sometimes it seems he only succeeds in enunciating four or five words a day. In reply to questions from outsiders he answers 'yes' or 'no'. Often he simply doesn't answer. His lips tremble slightly at the corners, his mouth opens as though a reply is forthcoming, one waits for the reply – and nothing comes out. Adam simply shuts his lips and continues to gaze steadily at one. In spite of what one may suppose, he isn't a shy child. Often this silence is because he cannot think of an appropriate answer, and no answer is preferable to an imprecise one. You ask him, for instance, does he prefer

Mozart to Beethoven? His mouth opens – a long pause – and then finally – no reply. While most children would name one composer or the other simply to please the adult addressing him, or so as to make conversation, Adam thinks such a question is a deadly serious matter, one which needs deep reflection and one for which he doesn't have an immediate answer. So he doesn't reply.

On the rare occasions when Adam does get round to speaking, his voice is thin and seems to emanate from three or four feet behind his head. 'No,' he says, 'Yes,' he says, with a finality and a meaning which these common words seldom seem to acquire in normal conversation.

Perhaps he is so taciturn because he speaks with his hands. His devotion to the piano is as fierce as Christian's to mathematics. His concentration when he is playing the piano is steely, the sights which he sets himself are the highest possible. For Adam the most important thing in the world is to play the piano and to play it well. Every evening when he comes home from school, he goes upstairs to his bedroom, often looking neither to right nor left, to start on a gruelling evening of selfless practice.

His is a touching room. The floor is bare except for a small rug, there is an iron bedstead, rather high for a child, and leaning against it a bicycle with a puncture which nobody seems to have got round to mending. Around the room there are a few books, an elderly wireless set now in pieces, a home-built toy, some paintings stuck to the wall and a heap of sheet music. In the middle of it stands his piano – perhaps the most valuable single object in the house, a highly polished upright with a seat set surprisingly high for so small a child. It is the kind of piano advertisers like to see glowing with wax, a suburban child seated on its stool in a tasteful lounge. Somehow it looks out of place in Adam's cluttered room.

Adam is so small he can scarcely reach the pedals. Furthermore, since he doesn't like shoes, he is often clad in carpet slippers, his toes prodding delicately down towards the pedals. No sooner is he perched on the seat than he begins to play, at once totally wrapped in the music in front of him. Sometimes he will practise for three or four hours an evening, stopping only to drink a hardly noticed glass of orange juice Maria brings up to him, coming down reluctantly for supper, playing each piece of music until he is perfectly satisfied. Some evenings he invites the rest of the family to come and listen to him play, arranging concerts for them. These are intensely serious events. None of the children talk or rustle, the atmosphere is as solemn as an important night at the Wigmore Hall. But Adam seems to be as happy when he is performing for his family as when he is practising for himself, absorbing himself totally in the music in either case. While he is conscious of the audience, he is as rapt as when alone, and as evidently conscious of the high seriousness of the event of making music. On such occasions Adam is immensely dignified – but it is a shade ridiculous that so small, so touchingly frail a child, should conduct himself with such open gravity.

Adam was an average baby, but as he grew older he seemed to have the greatest difficulty in expressing himself or communicating with the other human beings. In the commune where his mother was struggling against extreme circumstances to bring up her children, Adam seemed unable to get enough of her attention. She was desperately worried – in comparison to Christian her new child seemed terribly backward. Could it be, she wondered, that he was retarded, or damaged? It was true Adam was listless, uninterested, unable to cope with communicating with other children and adults.

Maria reacted with characteristic firmness. If there was anything wrong with Adam it was the environment. He must be taken away – the then charged and over-emotional atmosphere of the commune was clearly affecting her son's development. He needed not special treatment, but the special kind of attention that only his mother could give, and this only when she was free from other cares. Even though their departure would hasten the inevitable collapse of the commune, Maria and Martin left it.

No sooner were the family out of the commune and in their refuge up the hill in the comparative calm of the cottage than Maria started to wrestle with Adam's problem, much as a medieval mystic wrestled with the devil. Hour by hour she would sit with him, coax him, talk to him, bring him out of himself, try to erase from his mind the hostility and emotionally overcharged atmosphere that he had clearly begun to find so overpowering among the adults with whom he had passed his earliest months in the commune down in the valley. Progress was very slow. Adam would sit and stare out of the window for hours, or would abstractedly gather stones, or simply gaze gravely at his mother from out of his wide grey eyes. But Maria persevered, seizing gratefully on the least signs of active participation, waiting patiently, as she believed she must, for the time Adam would once more feel that he should attempt life. Maria knew deep in her heart that Adam would pull through, and she never for one instant gave up hope. And at about three and a half he started painting, and his conduct began to become more liberated.

Then on his fifth birthday came the turning point – Adam announced that he wanted as a birthday present a toy piano that he had seen in Woolworths. A poor wooden thing, it had only a handful of jarring half-tuned notes. But now instead of gazing abstractedly, Adam sat in the evenings picking out tunes on his new toy, almost as any child would. This incessant picking, too distracting to be tolerated by the adult members of the average family, seemed to give him pleasure, to help him find a deeply calming inner fulfilment. Maria saw here the first signs of a door opening onto his mind, an area in which she could lead him to excel in the way that the seven-year-old Christian was already excelling in mathematics.

She encouraged him, and now Adam spent hours picking out simple tunes, always with his mother tactfully helping him onwards. Christian says, jokingly, that there is no justice in the world because he could pick out better tunes than Adam did then.

But for Adam his toy piano was a revelation. Here was something at which he could excel – and which didn't necessitate the risks inherent in too much speech, or in competition with Christian. The latter was tactfully discouraged from competing and Adam's progress continued.

Maria and Martin decided that Adam should be given a full-sized piano as a present. One was unearthed in the local junk shop, and shipped up the hill to the cottage. It cost £12. Adam longed to play it, but his desire was unequal to the technical problems of reading and understanding music, and his hands were too small to bridge notes on the piano which lay so maddeningly silent.

Maria wasn't daunted. This was a problem which she could overcome. Although her knowledge of musical theory was slight, her love of music was considerable. At home in Italy she had sometimes sat for hours listening to string quartets with her friends, trying to discover in the music of Beethoven the peace and meaning which she had found so hard to find before she met Martin. She had decided that if that was what he desired, Adam was going to be a musician. It was only a question of stirring the talents that she knew lay in him. A teacher was found in the village. He was, however, shy and diffident, and confronted by this intense and silent child, would only say to Adam, 'Wonderful, wonderful,' whatever the child did. Adam, with the high intellectual standards of his family, found this more deeply insulting than being constantly corrected.

His lessons languished into silence. Adam didn't seem to be making the progress of which Maria thought he was capable. Clearly she saw that she must take a direct part in the teaching process.

Drawing on her Montessori training, she set about devising ways of helping Adam to master the formal rudiments of music. Cardboard notes were cut out and stuck onto giant models of the piano keyboard, and then related to the staves in printed music. Sometimes in the evenings memory games were played with the model stave. Progress was good. Then a game was invented – Maria was Mummy Tortoise, Adam was Adam Hare. The tortoise went slowly when it played on the keys – but the hare went quickly, leaping over whatever obstacles might be in its path. Adam began to gain new confidence – the hare sped out ahead of the tortoise. And his mother's scant knowledge of musical theory was in itself a help – often she was learning in tandem with Adam, making the joy of discovery a shared one.

Hours they sat together at the piano, sometimes playing together, sometimes Maria singing, and Adam accompanying her. Adam began to master the instrument, and his whole personality began to blossom. Now he could find an outlet with his hands that compensated for his difficulty in communicating in other ways. Of an evening he would play for his siblings improvised but formal concerts – and he began to take a far fuller part in the life of the family.

The word began to get around the Welsh valleys that in a small village there was a phenomenal child capable of playing the piano better than any child had played for many generations. Maria and Martin decided he must now go to the best teacher in the village, even though the fees would be a terrible strain on their restricted budget. This worthy gentleman lived on the better side of the village, beyond the spoil heaps in a neat terraced house painted copper red up to a plimsoll line three feet above the dusty pavement, the doorway set off by a doorstep so clean you could almost see your face in it. He was D. T. Davies, conductor of the local choir, possessor of the MBE for services to Welsh choral singing, known to all and sundry in the village as 'D.T.' – and much quoted in the local paper as an oracle on all things musical.

He was a worthy man, a fine working musician in the great tradition of Welsh choral singing. Unfortunately, by nature D.T. was as taciturn as Adam. For hours they would sit in total silence. Adam would play, D.T. would listen. There would be a long silence. D.T. would make one or two marks on the score. Adam would play it again – perfectly. There would be a long silence. Then D.T. would hand a fresh score to Adam. Adam would go away again – next week he would play it perfectly. D.T. would sit in silence. Adam would play it again and so on.

Sometimes the silences would go on so long that Mrs Davies would look in to see if the lesson was over and Adam had gone home. But if it was negative as a teaching relationship, as a musical lending library it was positive. The child got better and better and his fame spread further among the local communities.

Then one day a circular arrived at Adam's school advertising a national junior piano-playing contest – a contest open to all the children in Britain. The competitors would come from the famous specialist schools and the most famous teachers in the length and breadth of the land. The upper age limit was eighteen – and there was a substantial prize. Adam, aged seven, decided he was going to enter in the thirteen-and-under group. D.T. was against it.

'There'll be questions,' he said, 'people will ask where you came from, who taught you. I don't want to be bothered.'

But Adam was resolute. He informed his parents – didn't consult them, simply made a characteristically direct statement – and they too thought it might upset him and reverse his new progress.

'Why do you want to enter?' his parents asked him.

Said Adam: 'I want to hear other people play. I have never heard the other children play and I want to hear them make proper music.'

The heats were held in Cardiff. Adam won easily, the other children seemed simply not to be of the same standard. And Adam was bitterly disappointed – not because he had won, but because the standard of the other playing he had heard failed to give him the pleasure and knowledge he felt he should have been able to gain from older and more experienced players. He returned to his own twelve-pound piano and began to prepare the set piece at his silent lessons with D.T.

The finals were held in the Festival Hall, London, before a panel of distinguished judges. The great hall was packed with a crowd of dinner-jacketed celebrities and proud parents. It was an occasion of grandeur and social splendour unknown in the Welsh village. Adam didn't appear to notice the crowd and once more he was disappointed, this time because he was unable to hear the other competitors. Each was kept out of sight and hearing of the others until his turn came to play. Adam played his set piece with composure – as though he was playing to his family. When it was all over the judges called out the winners in reverse order – first of all the third prize winner, second the second, finally the first. Adam had won. He went up to receive his prize uncomprehendingly, oblivious of what had happened, since he thought that as he was the third person to be called onto the platform, he must be third in the contest. A celebratory dinner was arranged, and Quaker friends took Martin, who had brought his son up for the occasion, and Adam out for a meal. Adam sat silently throughout the dinner. Then the friends said: 'The time has come to ring up your mother and tell her you have won.'

'Won?' said Adam. 'No, I only came third.'

They tried to persuade him he had won.

'I can't have won – to win you have to be very good.'

To persuade him of his victory they showed him his cheque for £200.

'Aren't you proud of winning?' they said.

'No,' said Adam, 'I don't think it was important to win. It was important to play well.'

From Adam these words were not a vain boast, or a piece of false modesty, they were a simple statement of truth.

A certain amount of publicity surrounds the winners of such prizes, but Adam, all offers of performances turned down, returned to the house set high on the Welsh hills, and in no time he had been forgotten except by the local villagers. They now began to look with new eyes at the family as they did their shopping in the local town, neat and tidy, but slightly odd-looking and apart in their usually home-made clothes. Mothers would talk behind Maria's back, and sometimes one of the bolder ones would come up to her and say 'Isn't your little boy sweet?' and kiss the mutely protesting Adam on the cheek. It was an inconvenience, but something the family, with the possible exception of Adam, put up with resignedly.

Adam's prize didn't change his way of life. He still went to the primary school where Christian had been so unhappy. No one there took any more interest in the second son than they had taken in his eldest brother, the headmaster not even bothering to congratulate Adam on winning such an important prize. He still went to his lessons with D. T. Davies and still practised three or four hours a day upstairs on the piano. But it was becoming increasingly apparent that the schooling available in the village was almost more unsatisfactory in Adam's case than it had been in Christian's.

Christian had needed specialised teaching in mathematics, but that could have been provided by correspondence – all a budding mathematician needs is a pen and a slide-rule – while a pianist has to have constant stimulation and instruction. And there is no lower age limit for pianists – the younger they start to play the better. Delay can cost a career. And Adam had quite literally never played with other children in the musical sense. He had never been part of an orchestra, had never played piano duets with anybody but his teacher – his mother was incapable, his brothers and sister were involved in other things. If he was to be a serious concert pianist – and an increasingly large number of people agreed that he had the potential – he must receive the specialised musical training which is so necessary for musical children.

If Christian burns with a cold blue flame of pure intellect, Adam burns with a pure and passionate flame of will, so strong that nothing will turn him from his chosen aim to become a concert pianist. In a young child such dedication may seem faintly ridiculous, such high seriousness suspect. But an aquaintance with Adam soon stills such doubts.

His gifts are as lopsided in their way as Christian's. Adam was nine when he won the contest – in most of his school work he was only average, while in piano playing he had the skill and maturity and, above all, the poise and technical assurance of a gifted student perhaps seven or eight years older than himself. Nevertheless he was still dependent on his mother for all the things a child of his age is dependent for – in some ways more so than other children, for he was very close to Maria. Above all, his relationship with his brothers and sister, especially the latter, was vitally important to him. His parents couldn't bring themselves to uproot him and send him away to board somewhere, as would be necessary were he to go to one of the specialised music schools like the Menuhin School or the Bath and Wells Choir School.

It was a deadlock. Characteristically it was resolved by Adam himself. One day he announced: 'I want to go away to school.' At the prospect of losing perhaps the most fragile of her children, Maria's heart was wrung, and Martin too found it hard to accept. But such is the family atmosphere that Adam's decision was accepted without debate or question. His voice in his own affairs was as powerful as any other voice in the family, and as worthy of respect as either his father's or his mother's. So nobody tried to cajole him, nobody tried to make him change his mind, nobody pointed out the difficulties of going away to school. Adam had made up his mind. The data had been presented to him, and he wanted to go regardless of the sacrifices. With heavy hearts Maria and Martin set about making the arrangements.

Fortunately the local council decided it would pay the bill. In a sense it was for them an expiation of the troubles and difficulties they had caused the family when, years before, they had threatened Maria with a court action on the grounds of failing to educate her children. Now the towns-people were proud of their musical son – proud in a Welsh way of education and prowess in music and song; proud that they could still prove superior to the richer and more industrialised parts of the British Isles in the things that really mattered. A school was selected in Manchester – the Royal Hospital School – a blue-coat school. A scholarship was obtained, a uniform bought, sensible shoes, and neatly labelled handkerchiefs carefully gathered and packed by Maria – and Adam left home to go to school.

He was an unusual schoolboy, grave and composed, the wardrobe the council had provided somehow slightly too large and too 'sensible' for him. He stood, gazing from his grave eyes at the school playground – even more unusual in attitude to his new school than in appearance. He had, he felt, come to play the piano for them, to learn about music fully and seriously. It was *they* who must accommodate themselves to him. Such – to him – quite rational idiosyn-crasies as refusal to wear heavy school shoes, eat school food, or keep to a timetable restricting the four hours practice he was accustomed to each day would just have to be tolerated by the adult authorities. There was no room even for debate, he was not intending to change his attitude. The school gulped – and to their great credit complied; not that they really had much choice. This boy, they came to see, meant 'no' when he said 'no', and 'yes' as literally. What he did not mean was 'no until you beat me, keep me in and give me lines' – it was an absolute attitude – and, outside the special ethos of his family circle, a rare one for a nine-year-old. His practice hours, his permission to attend Quaker meetings, and his need to wear slippers most of the time were vital to him, and that was that. What became clear at school was that everything was really an adjunct of his piano-playing – it was not just an activity, it was a central part of life itself.

Apart from school, Adam acquired a teacher – for a pianist far more important than a wife, and almost as binding and as permanent a relationship. Fanny Waterman – perhaps the best known specialist piano teacher in England – took him on. An extravert, she conceives and performs each lesson in her splendid house as though she were on a stage. She cries, she bounds over to the piano, she plays, she dances. During their first lesson, Adam observed the torrent much as though he were suddenly confronted by a being from outer space.

'What,' demanded Fanny, 'is the difference between the way I do it and yours?'

'You,' said Adam, his voice coming from four feet behind his head, 'played a wrong note.' It was a simple statement – neither a criticism nor a point scored. Fanny carried on – ignoring the fact that most of her questions elicited no replies – seeing that this strange but immensely gifted pupil could answer her largely with his hands. As the weeks went by, progress in what is an essentially slow business, was more than satisfactory. Between Fanny, an immensely gifted teacher, and Adam, as gifted a child, a relationship has begun which will develop over a period of years, and one which promises greater things.

Outside his music, Adam shows signs of the intellect he undoubtedly shares with Christian. He has a game, calculated to humiliate the unwary adult, called 'Capitals'.

'Will you play capitals?' he asks suddenly from out of his usual silence. 'What is the capital of Spain? Of Russia? Of the Republic of Chad? Of China? Of the Dutch West Indies?'

Those who progress beyond this point have to contend with: 'What is the population density of the Cameroons – or the fourth largest city in China?' Adam knows it all – answers unhesitatingly and, the subject exhausted, relapses into silence. Except when with his siblings, for then he too will play complex games with Paul – or with Ruth, for whom he composes pieces they can play together, she performing on her flute.

Of all the children, Adam fits in best with what has become the popular image of 'genius' – surely anyway not a word that is ever appropriate to a young child. He is introverted, committed to his art with a passion quite uncommon at his age, and furthermore views himself and his talents with utter seriousness. Given, as he has been, the best of teachers and the maximum of Maria's support, and divorced from the pressure of constantly having to succeed, Adam stands at the threshold of a major artistic career. It is an opportunity born of his mother's determination, a toy piano, and his fierce talent and innate musicality.

CHAPTER SEVEN

PAUL AND RUTH

It is harder to form a clear picture of the potentialities of Maria's two younger children – both of them are still enveloped in Maria's prepared environment, and less of their final character and attainments can be perceived. At their age, Maria believes, they are still subject to sudden bursts of progress and long periods of delay. She is not discouraged by the latter, but they make it difficult to produce any sort of meaningful progress report on Paul and Ruth – at any moment of writing they may seem impossibly advanced, as with Paul's grasp of mathematics, or fairly ordinary.

Ruth is a miniature carbon copy of her mother – the same perfectly oval face, the same dark eyes and the same hair drawn severely back from her forehead. Her looks are those of the grave, beautiful girls who gaze so serenely out of the frame of a Renaissance painting. Unlike her brothers, who seem gawky or restrained, Ruth instantly gives an impression of warmth and concern for strangers, accepting them with a frankness and totality only possible in a child who has never suffered a rebuff. It is almost as though she is intent on warming with her femininity the cold intelligence of her elder brothers.

Like her mother, Ruth is too often bent on self-sacrifice, too often self-effacing when confronted by the formidable talents of her brothers. When she was about five, she showed a talent for ballet. Classes were found in a nearby village but the journey and expense proved a difficult additional burden for her mother. Seeing that this was so, Ruth gave up her lessons. Such spare cash and energy as there were, she felt, could be more fruitfully devoted to her brothers.

By inclination Ruth is closest to her brother Adam. When difficulties arise, she stands between him and a sometimes uncomprehending world, losing herself in the reflected joy of his talent. Ruth herself is moderately gifted musically, she plays the recorder well, and lately the flute, and sometimes joins with Adam in playing duets. But her main diversion is helping her mother – coping with household tasks, and thus allowing Maria more time free to tend to the more elaborate needs of her brothers.

Indeed, Ruth has always been especially close to her mother, presenting an oasis of calm among the difficulties which often seem to press in on Maria. Ruth almost never becomes flustered or rattled. Her mother, for her part, ascribes some of Ruth's calm and repose to the fact that she was allowed to stay at the breast until she gave it up of her own volition. Even now Ruth recalls having her 'acky' or 'sucky', as she called it, well up to her third birthday, and Maria believes this late abandonment of the breast played a central part in developing her daughter's temperament.

Whether this is true or not – Margaret Mead certainly agrees that there is some kind of connection – Ruth is an exceptionally serene and beautiful child. She came as a great additional strength to Martin and Maria when she was born. It was just after they had moved out of the town away from the community, and the strange isolation and special silences of the countryside still seemed unfamiliar and a little forbidding to them.

In the remote isolation of their cottage Ruth was born with a single hour of labour – and by the time the midwife came the only sound on the hillside was the bleating of newborn lambs. It was so peaceful, the nurse said, that nobody could believe that a baby had been born there that night. Like a Roman child born with auspicious omens, Ruth seems to have had peace and calm around her ever since. Of her, a Russian peasant might say, 'she is the little mother of the world'.

When one comes to assess the potential of Ruth, one sometimes feels that she is less gifted than her brothers – and in the purely academic sense this is true. It is only as one knows her better that one realises her potential gifts are of a softer and subtler nature – gifts of giving and of living, gifts that are especially strong in Maria.

These qualities arouse some fear for the future, for perhaps this warm purity makes Ruth potentially the most vulnerable when confronted by the outside world. A child who knows only how to give and to receive love may be in for a rude awakening. But if it is the purpose of 'the process' to propagate itself – then Ruth's children may well benefit hugely from what she has learned from her mother. And Maria herself believes that, not having had the uncertain and storm-tossed childhood that her mother endured, Ruth will be even stronger than she is when the path becomes stony.

Almost indivisible from Ruth is Paul. Since neither of them has yet had much formal school-time contact, per-force they spend most of their time together, seated with Maria at a low table littered with the paraphernalia of learning – their toys. When other children bicker and grumble about each other, Paul and Ruth are perfectly serene with each other – Ruth acting unselfconsciously as a 'little mother' to Paul, guarding and encouraging him in whatever activity he may attempt. It is a devotion which goes far beyond the conventional 'inseparable brother and sister'.

Even a brief acquaintance with Paul goes a long way to explain Ruth's devotion. Paul is five. He is physically a ravishingly attractive child, with rosy cheeks and blue eyes, and a shock of blond hair covering a domed forehead. Irrepressible, in that nobody has ever tried to repress him, Paul approaches life headlong.

His whole personality is almost literally bursting out of his five-year-old form. Paul never walks when he can run, never talks when he can shout, never sits still when he can be climbing something, never remains silent when he can be asking a question.

Paul is instantly curious with the curiosity of somebody who has never been told 'don't touch' or 'not now, I'm busy.' Maria has never restrained him from exploring a fascinating object on grounds of dirt or inconvenience. Only danger has been allowed to prevent him from doing what he wants, and then his mother has explained to him why he mustn't pursue his curiosity further, rather than simply forbidding him.

When film cameras were brought into his home, Paul reacted quite differently from his elder brothers and sister, who treated them with lofty disinterest. For Paul this was an opportunity for performance. He studied the camera, was tactfully restrained from dismantling it with his trusted screwdriver, and then complained that he felt it was not giving him sufficient attention.

'You're all giggling at me,' he would proclaim, giggling away himself. But so guileless was this exhibition that it disarmed even the hardened camera team, accustomed to less endearing types of exhibitionism.

For them Paul provided perhaps the purest example of the difference between his family and their own – brought up with their conventional parents in less isolated, suburban environments. Paul accidentally spilled some paint.

'Don't do that,' said the cameraman, and then, conscious that he mustn't frighten the child, 'it's naughty.'

'What's naughty mean?' asked Paul, in genuine curiosity. 'Naughty' was a word that he had simply never heard before.

The cameraman started to explain and found the grave eyes of a listening child, genuinely curious about this strange concept, so disarming that he ground to a halt. What did he really mean by naughty when he used it with his own children? Did they understand what he meant any better than Paul? For the cameraman it was a terrible moment of truth. Characteristically Maria came to his aid.

'It's only a shorthand,' she explained, 'to show that the child is allowing his curiosity to irritate his parent.'

Almost every passing woman succumbs to the seemingly irresistible temptation of hugging Paul. Tactically it is a mistake. Paul simply does not need the physical reassurance of friendly contact. A hand on the shoulder, a pat on the head are coldly received. He cannot even bring himself to kiss his mother – a lick like that of a wild animal seems his only overt sign of the affection in which he swims and breathes like a fish in water.

If Ruth has a special relationship with Adam, Paul has a special relationship with Christian. He adores his elder brother and wants only to emulate him. Sometimes he simply climbs on Christian so as to be closer. Christian, interrupted in reading a scientific paper, exclaims: 'Oh, oh!' in his lilting voice. But such is the family atmosphere that he never complains, and always unquestioningly gives up what he is doing to play with Paul as though his younger brother has an absolute right to his attention. For Paul he is prepared to spend hours playing complicated games of imagination, pursuing the imaginary Mr Badcat, or helping Paul paint a plastic model or finish a picture.

While these 'Badcat' games do not differ in intensity of imagination from those played by other children, their imagery reflects the extraordinary lack of overt violence which prevails in that house. At their most extreme these games resort to tickling, but sudden death and guns are unknown in confounding the imaginery forces of evil. Badcat is undone by superior forces of good rather than by extra-powerful evil or by violence in any form. Perhaps more remarkable still, this purity of play takes place without any overt control on Maria's part.

It was for Paul that Christian wrote his book, painted the pictures and wrote the poems. Paul repays the gift with an iron devotion, knows all the poems by heart, can recite them, or sing them, or shout them, or play them out. All in all. Paul is intent on growing up to be in every particular exactly like his elder brother.

Paul's education has been the purest and most controlled. Maria has benefited from the lessons she learned with her other children, by the peace engendered by the location, and by the stability the family has finally achieved. Additionally, now that the other children are often away at school she can give herself entirely to Paul.

It is a devotion that brooks no interruption, allows no diversion. When she is with Paul she asks not to be telephoned, tries not to answer the doorbell. It isn't simply that the moment of interruption may be the crucial second when a door to his mind opens, but she finds a diversion will often make it perversely difficult to pick up the threads.

Paul, at four and a half, repays her attention by displaying an almost boundless capacity for jumping the hurdles of primary education. Working with cardboard numbers which his mother and father have made him, he can add, multiply, divide. He has come to an understanding of fractions with a series of hardboard cut-outs representing a circular whole divided into slices like a cake – a standard, if home-built, Montessori aid. Paul is as interested in numbers as his eldest brother was.

'One is to three,' he remarked at an early lesson, 'as two is to six.'

One morning Paul woke me up, anxious to share a recently gained piece of knowledge.

'I have come,' he said, 'to see how much you know.'

It was very early. Without opening my eyes I replied: 'I know nothing.'

'Wake up! I've got a question for you. What is the difference between nought, and zero, and nothing?'

'They are all the same,' I said.

'No they are not,' said Paul triumphantly, 'nought is a measurement of negative mathematical quantity, zero is the same thing with decimals and nothing means nothing at all. That shows how little you know.'

It was a crushing defeat.

Naturally Christian was accused of teaching his younger brother this parrot-fashion.

'No,' said Christian. 'I *explained* it to him – if you can't understand about negative mathematical quantity, you will never understand a lot of things.' Which is doubtless true.

The frontiers of Paul's interest, however, are not limited to the intellectual. He is obsessed by the need to make sensual exploration of the things around him. His father responds to this challenge by keeping a box of discarded household objects – plugs, old radios, switches which can be endlessly taken to pieces and then reassembled. Paul will spend hours at this, armed with screw-driver and pliers, displaying remarkable manual dexterity. Aesthetically less pleasing than many educational toys, his box of old plugs seems to provide endless opportunity for sensual exploration of his environment. Now a remarkably swift progression to plastic aeroplane bits is taking place, making full use of and extending his manual dexterity in a way truly remarkable for a five year old.

This exploration through dismantling extends to new objects presented to him. When confronted by a television set in an hotel lounge, playing a situation comedy, Paul didn't laugh. His head slightly on one side, he gazed at it with total concentration for less than a minute. Then he went round the back to investigate.

'Can I take it to pieces?' he asked. Only the swift use of reason was able to restrain him from treating it the same way as his box of switches. Once he was persuaded it was genuinely dangerous he returned to painting – his back to the set, apparently uncurious about the comedians mouthing away on the screen. First-hand creation was clearly more interesting than second-hand experience. Perversely, the only machine which seems safe from his dismantling passion is a typewriter. The pleasure of composing words on it seems to outweigh the delights of taking it to pieces.

Viewed in terms of his potential, rather than of his already considerable achievement, Paul is truly extraordinary. It is clearly only a matter of time before he too abandons learning by touch, and from simple Montessori mathematical learning patterns, and starts to emulate Christian by taking up five figure logarithms or trying to disprove Kepler's law. In the meantime, he is trying to learn the violin, wants to know how to type, write poems, do geometry, collect stones and a thousand-and-one other things. While many children have vitality, Paul has a driving force that is almost primeval in its intensity. He is as pure in spirit as Ruth, but while she is warm and feminine, he is waiting only till his mind and body are just so much bigger before he too achieves something as startling as his elder brothers.

He combines the fierce intelligence of Christian with the inner fire of Adam, hampered by no inhibitions or rejections to bank down the fires which already burn with such phenomenal intensity. So far in his life he has only had to cope with one solitary frustration – that he is only five years old, which perforce imposes certain temporary limitations in regard to achievement. Paul means to set this to rights as soon as possible.

CHAPTER EIGHT

They say the best stories have a tidy ending – but the story of Maria and her children is perforce an incomplete one. It is partly this which gives it its fascination. Indeed, while this book was in preparation, there was an almost constant stream of visitors asking for news of the children, or advancing one reason or another for their exceptional talents. Few stayed less than an hour – and at its height it became necessary quite simply to refuse to discuss Maria and the children with friends. I only hope that this book will answer some of their questions.

In addition, professional interest took an exceptional time to die down. Even now the occasional journalist rings up to ask rather wistfully to be allowed to do a 'follow-up', or simply for Maria's address. They have been put off as tactfully as possible, as have the seemingly endless procession of teacher-training colleges, psychologists and just plain mothers who want Maria's advice or her presence at a function. Perhaps they, too, will find some of the answers they seek in these pages.

What gives this curious story its peculiar fascination? One has to ask the question. In part it is because the substance of Maria's process seems to strike a deep chord in everybody who has had to do with children – to arouse a feeling that 'had I been given opportunity, strength and sufficient money, or lack of attachment to money, I too could have done that'.

There is also the endlessly fascinating and quite unresolvable debate as to how much Maria's system has affected the development of her children. Are they, people ask, a genetic sport, or uniquely the products of 'the process'? The scientific answer seems to be that environment is responsible for only about twenty per cent in the finally developed capabilities of a person – the rest of us is governed by genetic inheritance. But this goes only a little way towards stilling the dark self-questioning of the part of us which feels instinctively that Maria is right, not only in abstract theory, but in achievement. For whatever the cause, or combined causes, of the remarkable talents of the children they are very clearly developing with extraordinary freedom and speed. When one exceptionally talented genecist at Cambridge was asked what her opinion of the phenomena was, she answered unhesitatingly 'If I were you I would keep away – it isn't natural.' From the point of view of providing rational and cut and dried answers, her reaction was probably the correct one.

Whatever else it is, this book is clearly only an interim report. The children change and develop daily, as all children do. In addition there will be changes resulting from a major alteration that has recently taken place in the lives of Maria and her children. For the family decided, about three months ago, to leave their isolation in Wales and, as it were, to rejoin the mainstream of society. Accordingly they have moved to a northern industrial city, setting up home in a red brick Victorian terrace in a slightly seedy section of the town. In place of the isolation – certainly rather austere, but peaceful – of the spoilheaps behind the Welsh village, now they are hemmed in by rows of identical houses crammed with working people better able to react to the latest programme on television than to the philosophy of Martin Buber. Inevitably the children will feel deprived of the countryside, and will meet contemporaries with very different cultural and moral patterns, and as inevitably Maria will find much of her time spent at grips with a modern, polluted urban jungle.

On the face of it, it was astonishing that she and Martin decided to abandon the painfully prepared environment and move to an industrial centre. But this decision too must be viewed in the context of Maria's fearless refusal to compromise with what she believes to be right, and her equally striking rejection of anything she believes has outlived its usefulness. Because the cottage in Wales had provided an ideal siting for the prepared environment was, in her opinion, no reason to become sentimentally attached to its brick-and-mortar reality.

Maria's first motive for uprooting the family and moving to the city was Adam – he needed the full-time attention of his piano teacher, and it was physically impossible for him to have it while they lived in Wales. As a stop-gap he went to boarding-school, but Maria felt that at nine he was still not sufficiently prepared to come to grips with the realities of the world outside the prepared environment – he was not, as it were, armour-plated. It was not that Adam had failed to 'settle in' at the boarding-school in the city. He had succeeded in cutting himself off from much of the life of the school behind a protective wall of silence, vocation and certainty. But divorced from his brothers and sister he was reluctant to emerge and relax, or even to play the piano, as he had before.

It was this which decided Maria and Martin to leave Wales and set up home nearer both school and teacher. It was not, Maria reasoned, an irrational step. The environment had served to steer all the children through their first five years. They were able, or would soon be able, to cope with the mainstream of society in doses, the size of which she believed she could still control in their new urban home.

Furthermore, isolation was having some undesirable effects, now that the children were old enough to want to make use of facilities available only in cities. Near their new home there would be museums and concerts, libraries and the company of other like-minded people.

And Maria had in the back of her mind the fact that in an urban community, she could once more be of service – minding babies, or helping in simple, often menial ways, with the social problems which teem in an industrial city. Martin, too, would be better able to make use of such qualifications as he possessed. No sooner was the rationale established than the move was made; rather suddenly, as usual with Maria's family.

In many ways Adam has seemed to adjust best to the move. He came home from school to his new home with relief. His piano was installed once more in an upstairs room, and he was welcomed back warmly by his siblings. Soon it was almost as though nothing had changed, the family sitting every evening as they had in Wales, while Adam played to them.

But now he was joined by Ruth – the move had coincided for her with a period of intense development. It was almost as if the extra effort of helping her mother cope with the multiple difficulties of the change had unlocked in her a force which spilled over into other creative activities. At her new school Ruth bloomed, painting and sewing with renewed grasp of shape and form. Her music began to improve with leaps and bounds – she took up the flute and was soon able to join Adam in the evening concerts. He would nurse her with infinite care through simple beginner's pieces, and then progressively lead her on to more difficult ones, acting like an experienced and especially sympathetic accompanist. From these sessions Adam has taken to writing music especially for Ruth to play. Carefully gauged for her skill on the flute, the pieces are based on family incidents which have caught his imagination – the day Ruth nearly got run over by a car, a pet bird that was attacked by the cat, and so on. They are not works of strong personality, but they show Adam's easy command of the resources of his instrument and his increasing curiosity in the process of composition, while in human terms they demonstrate his closeness to his sister, and provide a likely pointer as to the direction his creative impulses are likely to take.

Christian has taken to his new surroundings less happily than his brothers and sister. Superficially he might seem to be the one least attached to the Welsh countryside and the rural diversions that occupied his younger siblings, but he seems to be most at sea in the unfamiliar urban atmosphere.

Partly, Christian's difficulties spring from his early adolescence – at twelve the boy is springing up, his voice has broken and his already endearingly bizarre features are now set off by thick and appropriately professorial spectacles.

But only some of his problems spring from adolescence. Others may possibly be due to his new school, one of the most famous in the country. Here, instead of trying to make the special effort to assimilate Christian that his school in Wales did, they have tended to try bending the boy to fit the system, making perhaps too little allowance either for his precocity or for the almost unbelievable speed with which he seems to devour the conventional syllabus. This new school seemingly believes that since Christian already has his 'A' levels, the equivalent of university entrance, at twelve, he should for the time being abandon the subjects which he has mastered and devote himself to the arts subjects they feel he will need if he is to become in effect a 'whole man'. Accordingly his curriculum is now angled more towards classical and modern languages, history and literature.

Christian, however, is simply burning with curiosity about mathematics, only now instead of sympathy and a little warming admiration, he feels himself to be receiving at best lukewarm encouragement from his teachers. Very possibly the school is right, but it could become an unhappy state of affairs which will need resolving if Christian is not going to become frustrated during the time he must wait before he is able to go to university – presumably at about sixteen. Only four years away, as people tell Christian with relish – but that is a lifetime away when one is only twelve.

Paul on the other hand is flourishing. At present he is deeply interested in mathematics. Aided by Christian, he has taken to writing out his sums in Foltran, the computer language. It makes them incomprehensible to the outsider, but – so Christian assures one – will be of the greatest assistance to his brother when he comes face to face with a true computer in a year or two. Equally uncanny is Paul's new pocket toy.

'Would you like to see my computer?' he demands as one is walking down the street, and produces from his pocket the sort of calculator much used by psephologists on election programmes.

'Ask me a sum,' he cries.

'Multiply 123 by 6.'

'No – something *proper* – like the square root of 137,248' – a result he promptly proceeds to provide.

Educationalists often write that growing up is an adventure. For Paul this is quite literally true. Furthermore for him it is an exciting and fruitful adventure in which his side always comes out on top.

Maria presides over all of them exactly as she did when they were younger – still controlling the environment, still carefully encouraging each child in its disparate needs. She knows that for her the future can only mean that one by one they will take to the world outside, until even Paul has gone to try himself in comparison with those brought up in the rough-and-tumble of a more conventional upbringing. Maria has no doubts about the results – that tempered in the fire of love her children will prevail.

When Christian, Adam, Ruth and Paul have tried their wings, and found they can fly, then Maria plans that her life will enter a new phase. She intends to return to the studies that were interrupted fifteen years ago at Rome University. Only this time, instead of Greek philology she will study child psychology and philosophy. And Maria will have time, she believes, to devote herself to making a contribution to the community – something she feels she has perforce neglected while her own children were growing up. Having been of service to her family, Maria plans to be of service to others.

But all this lies in the future – it will be ten years before the process is over and all four children are out in the world. Until that time, this is a continuing story.

Publisher and author agree that it would be unforgivable to publish this story if, as a result, the family's privacy was invaded and Maria, Martin and the children were disturbed in any way. Names have therefore been changed, and they have undertaken not to betray the family's identity or whereabouts to anyone.